Community Works

Community Works

The Revival of Civil Society in America

E.J. DIONNE JR.
Editor

Brookings Institution Press
Washington, D.C.

About Brookings

The Brookings Institution is a private nonprofit organization devoted to research, education, and publication on important issues of domestic and foreign policy. Its principal purpose is to bring knowledge to bear on current and emerging policy problems, The Institution was founded on December 8, 1927, to merge the activities of the Institute for Government Research, founded in 1916, the Institute of Economics, founded in 1922, and the Robert Brookings Graduate School of Economics and Government, founded in 1924.

The Institution maintains a position of neutrality on issues of public policy. Interpretations or conclusions in Brookings publications should be understood to be solely those of the authors.

THE BROOKINGS INSTITUTION
1775 Massachusetts Avenue, N.W., Washington, D.C. 20036

Library of Congress Cataloging-in-Publication data

Community works : the revival of civil society in America / E.J. Dionne, editor.
p. cm.
Includes bibliographical references and index.
ISBN 0-8157-1868-3 (cloth : alk. paper)
1. Civil society—United States. 2. Community organization—United States. I. Dionne, E.J.
JC336.C835 1998
306'.0973—ddc21 98-19685
CIP

9 8 7 6 5 4 3 2 1

The paper used in this publication meets the minimum requirements of the American National Standard for Information Sciences—Permanence of Paper for Printed Library Materials: ANSI Z39.48-1984.

Typeset in Adobe Garamond

Composition by Cynthia Stock
Silver Spring, Maryland

Illustration by Maria Sese Paul
Silver Spring, Maryland

Printed by R. R. Donnelley & Sons Co.
Harrisonburg, Virginia

For Lucie-Anne, Drew, and Kim
For Brian, Rory, and Caitlin
And in memory of Peggy Boyle

Acknowledgments

AMONG THE many people who have helped me with this book are two who have been involved from the beginning. Brenda Szittya, editor of the *Brookings Review*, encouraged me to guest edit an issue of the *Review*, on the subject of civil society, and it was her generous advice, good humor, and wise editing that nudged that issue onto the path that led to this book. Kristen Lippert-Martin managed the transition from magazine to book with the intelligence, attention, grace, and wit that characterize all her work for the Brookings Governmental Studies program. She has a special gift of entering the minds of others, whether or not she agrees with them. It was a joy and an education to work with both Brenda and Kristen.

My thanks to each of the authors who responded with great enthusiasm and hard work to the idea of this collection. Special thanks to Bill Galston for his many insights. As executive director of the National Commission on Civic Renewal, Bill kindly granted us permission to adapt the papers presented to the commission by Bill Schambra and Theda Skocpol. For permission to reprint or adapt articles, thanks also to *Dissent* magazine, the *Weekly Standard*, and HarperCollins. And thanks to John Carr of the U.S. Catholic Conference for a tape of an address by the Reverend Eugene Rivers that laid the basis for his piece here. And our gratitude to the authors in this volume who participated in our civil society discussion in

September 1997 and to Senator Paul Wellstone and Bill Kristol for offering thoughtful responses to their work.

The partnership between Brookings and the Institute for Civil Society has been a blessing. Heartfelt thanks to Pam Solo and Gail Pressberg for support, for a stream of good ideas, and for their work on behalf of civil society.

My personal thanks to Michael Armacost, president of the Brookings Institution, and to Tom Mann, director of the Brookings Governmental Studies program, for bringing me here. Mike has been generously supportive of this project from the beginning, and Tom, a dear friend, has insights, energy, and warmth to spread around—and he does so generously. John DiIulio is a dynamo and an inspiration. Thanks also to my colleagues Bob Katzmann, Margaret Weir, Steve Hess, Pietro Nivola, Chris Foreman, Kent Weaver, Sarah Binder, Don Kettl, Bill Frenzel, Susan Stewart, Judy Light, Tara Ragone, Cindy Terrels, Pat Fowlkes, Laurel Imig, Wendy Schiller, and Jacob Hacker. Particular thanks to Susan for good advice at crucial moments, and to Tara for her many acts of thoughtful generosity.

The Brookings Press was enthusiastic about this book from the beginning, thanks to Bob Faherty. Susan Woollen combines a genius for design with an infectious sense of community that invites all to share in the creative process. Theresa Walker and Jill Bernstein helped make the book happen. Allegra Gatti sat down with Jill and created its wonderful title.

Finally, thanks to my wife, Mary Boyle, and to my children, James, Julia, and Margeaux, for reminding me why this subject matters and for teaching me about it every day. Thanks to Mary for good advice on the content of this book, and to James and Julia for wise counsel on the cover. Margeaux was too young to consult, but I suspect she'll like it, too.

E.J.D.

Contents

Community Works

1

Introduction

Why Civil Society? Why Now?

E.J. DIONNE JR.

"CIVIL SOCIETY" sounds so nice that few people can believe something serious lies behind the debate the idea has provoked.

Sometimes, the word "civil" is given pride of place and the phrase is taken to mean a society where people treat each other with kindness and respect, avoiding the nastiness we have come to associate with thirty-second political ads and a certain kind of televised brawl.

More formally, civil society refers to an array of fine institutions that nobody can possibly be against: churches that run teen pregnancy and after-school programs, neighborhood crime watch groups, Boy Scouts and Girl Scouts, Little Leagues, book clubs, veterans groups, Shriners, and Elks. What's to fight about? Putting aside the problem of overly zealous parent-fans, how many people are prepared to take the negative side of The Little League Argument?

And the phrase is further blessed by its association with the brave people in Eastern Europe who used it in their struggle against communism. Living under dictatorships, they discovered that even the most efficient police states could not stamp out all vestiges of independent social life that survived in cafes and churches and workplaces and families. The Eastern European rebels used these enclaves of civil society to incubate free societies that ultimately triumphed.

Not only does the civil society idea meet with skepticism because of its almost impossibly wholesome associations; it also arouses sensible suspicion because every side wants to use it for its own purposes. "Some ideas fail because they never make the light of day," Alan Wolfe argues in these pages. "The idea of civil society, many critics charged, failed because it became too popular."

Wolfe rightly finds this an insufficient indictment of the idea, but it's worth asking nevertheless: why is the civil society concept so popular? Why are so many scholars counting up how many organizations we belong to? Why do Little Leagues and churches seem to matter so much now to citizens, scholars, and politicians whose concerns ran elsewhere a decade ago? Why is so much passion invested in arguments over whether or not civil society is on the decline—whether, in Robert Putnam's now famous phrase, more of us are "bowling alone"? Why is so much hope being invested in the voluntary sector?

The civil society debate is not a flash in the pan or a fashionable attempt to transcend ideological and partisan conflicts by ignoring them. This book is offered in the belief that the civil society idea has gained currency because it responds both to practical problems that concern citizens and to intellectual difficulties encountered by serious thinkers all along the political spectrum.

As Michael Walzer argues here, the interest in civil society is rooted partly in honest self-criticism by people left, right, and center willing to face evidence that may be inconvenient to their own arguments. It reflects as well a widespread sense that changes in the economy and in the organization of work, family, and neighborhood have outpaced—if, one can hope, only temporarily—the capacity of older forms of civic and associational life to help individuals and communities cope. And it arises from an antigovernment mood that has been part of American life since the late 1970s. The interest in civil society reflects (for conservatives and libertarians) a reaction against government and (for liberals and progressives) a search for stronger ground on which to rebuild responsive and energetic government.

The civil society idea has been used for many purposes, so it is subject to many definitions. The definition that runs through this book is straightforward, summarized well by Benjamin Barber in his book, *A Place for Us.*

Civil society is "an independent domain of free social life where neither governments nor private markets are sovereign." It is "a realm we create for ourselves through associated common action in families, clans, churches and communities." It is a "third sector" that "mediates between our specific individuality as economic producers and consumers and our abstract collectivity as members of a sovereign people." Civil society is made up of the organizations and places where everyone knows your name, and probably a good many other things about you, and your commitments, and your family. It encompasses, as Walzer writes, "the networks through which civility is produced and reproduced."

The title of this book consciously links the academic debate over civil society with the popular desire to build—and rebuild—community. As Adam Seligman rightly notes in *The Idea of Civil Society*, civil society has been "used as a political slogan to advance the cause of community" and to challenge philosophies of radical individualism. Some of the arguments advanced here have points in common with the concerns of communitarian thinkers such as Michael Sandel and Amitai Etzioni, even if many of the authors do not think of themselves as communitarians. Most of these essays aspire to demonstrate that the idea of community works on a philosophical level, and to report that many community works are being performed by people who don't much care whether they are labeled "communitarian" or not. You don't have to be communitarian to care about community. You don't have to engage in the debate over civil society to build it.

But if a society wants to encourage those who are engaged in the hard work of forging community bonds, of building civil society, it needs to be aware of how important that work is and to honor those who do it.

The Roots of an Idea

The precursor to today's civil society debate was the discussion engendered by an important essay published in 1977 called *To Empower People.* Written by Peter Berger and Rev. Richard John Neuhaus, it made the case for "mediating structures"—organizations and associations that "mediated" between "the individual in his private life and the large institutions of public life." The mediating structures they had in mind were church, family, neighborhood, and voluntary associations. Their point was that, at a minimum, government should not undercut mediating structures and, better yet, where possible try to strengthen and support them. The mediating structures idea did not arise in a vacuum. It reflected a bubbling up, similar to today's interest in civil society, of a concern for neighborhood life and the discovery that rumors of the death of older forms of community had been greatly exaggerated. In important books such as *Unsecular Man* and *Why Can't They Be Like Us?*, Father Andrew Greeley captured this spirit by pointing out that we were more religious than we thought we were, and more interested in neighborhood sociability and ethnic attachments than the dominant upper middle class ethos would have us believe.

Berger and Neuhaus explicitly criticized liberals for a tendency "to be blind to the political (as distinct from private) functions of mediating structures." Liberalism's "main feature," Berger and Neuhaus asserted, was "a commitment to government action toward greater social justice within the existing system." This, in turn, translated into a reluctance to consider how an agenda for social justice might be more effectively pursued through associations independent of government.

The Berger-Neuhaus thesis gave conservatives a powerful framework for their criticisms of the welfare state, and it is part of the inspiration for the program outlined here by Senators Dan Coats and Rick Santorum. Politically, it could be seen as the manifesto of the "Reagan Democrat" who still felt the tug of some of the New Deal's social commitments but warmed to Reagan's invocations of "family, work, and neighborhood."

But the mediating structures idea also led liberals to self-criticism. Liberals, or at least many of them, came to accept (as Daniel Patrick Moynihan had argued in less receptive times) that the situation of the poor had worsened because of family breakdown, neighborhood violence, and a weakening of traditional local institutions and restraints. Social policies needed to address not only material poverty but also crime, drug addiction, the rise of the single-parent family—most broadly, the question of how values are generated and passed along to children.

For liberals, this did not mean abandoning economic explanations for the situation of the inner city. William J. Wilson's arguments about the high cost of economic change to the poor, especially impoverished black men, still resonate. But it did mean accepting that economic explanations were not sufficient. This led to a search for solutions that involved not only government, but, well, "mediating structures," including churches and families. If a new focus of social policy was to be how to promote "values" and "personal responsibility," social institutions outside government would have to be mobilized.

The civil society argument took another turn in the early 1990s that should be credited in large part to Alan Wolfe's argument in his pathbreaking book *Whose Keeper?* Wolfe closed the circle that Berger and Neuhaus began to draw. If liberals had been insufficiently attentive to the ways in which government impinged on the institutions of civil society, conservatives were not attentive enough to how the workings of the economic market could disrupt neighborhoods and family life—a point made forcefully here by Alan Ehrenhalt.

Wolfe argued that civil society needed to be protected from both the government and the economic market. He also argued that both democratic government and a free economy depend on virtues and values generated neither by the state nor by the market, but by civil society. In this, he paralleled arguments made by Daniel Bell in *The Cultural Contradictions of Capitalism*. As for individuals, Wolfe noted that we live neither "in government" nor "in the market," but in this third sphere defined by friendships, loyalties, love, and personal values (such as altruism and intimacy), which only occasionally characterize market or political relationships.

American conservatism has always been an amalgam of free market individualism and more communally minded traditionalism. Until recently, the individualist strain had been in the ascendency. But in the late 1990s, a significant group of conservatives rediscovered the traditionalist vocation of pointing to the problems of individualism and the imperfections of capitalism. They have rediscovered, in the words of Robert Nisbet, one of this century's most discerning conservative thinkers, that "neither moral values nor fellowship nor freedom can easily flourish apart from diverse communities, each capable of enlisting the loyalties of its members."

As Paul Starobin has documented in the *National Journal*, many conservatives have come to agree that capitalism, all by itself, will not produce what they see as "good values," and may, at times, promote what they would call "bad values." William Bennett's critique of Hollywood, for example, led him to a broader argument about what the market doesn't do. "Unbridled capitalism is a problem," Bennett said at the National Press Club in 1996. "It may not be a problem for production, but it's a problem for human beings. It's a problem for the whole dimension of things we call the realm of values and human relationships."

Starobin specifically ascribed the new questioning of pure capitalism to "conservatives active in what is known as the civil society movement." Such conservatives, he said, "are beginning to talk about modern capitalism in much the same terms as they discuss Big Government—as a disruptive, intrusive, morally untethered force that can rend the fabric of community life."

The argument of these conservatives is not anticapitalist. It is a statement about capitalism's limits. It is also about the limits of a conservative strategy that sees dismantling government as the way to help the poor. Conservatives such as Senator Coats and David Kuo have argued that if their philosophical allies hope to reduce the role of government, they will have to find ways to strengthen other sectors that are public but not governmental. Thus civil society.

Seen as a vehicle for self-criticism by both liberals and conservatives, the civil society idea might be summarized as an assertion that we will not be "saved" by either the market or the government. If that minimum level of agreement is reached, where does the argument go from there?

The Problem of Nostalgia

As both Alan Wolfe and Jean Bethke Elshtain note in their essays, many critics of the civil society idea see it as a form of nostalgia, a longing for the warm, encompassing (and closed) communities of the premodern era. Both rightly reject this criticism, but see it as leading to a truth about the civil society idea: it is the assertion of a group of people who think that contemporary society is missing something.

The "something" that is missed is defined in different ways by different people. Parents feel they are missing time with their children by spending too much time at work. Residents of crime-ridden neighborhoods miss the street corner and doorstep sociability made possible by physical security. People who move several times to get better jobs miss the continuity, familiarity, and sense of loyalty that come from long-time residence in a stable neighborhood. Employees sense less loyalty from their employers after the recent waves of "downsizing" and "right sizing." Members of a professional elite worry that too much of their social life is organized around what they do. Parents worry that they have lost control as values are transmitted to their children by outside forces, especially television.

In all these worries, there is, of course, a hint of nostalgia. Parents have always worried about where their children pick up values. We've had crime waves before. Americans have always been on the move and in search of new opportunities. What is a warm and stable neighborhood to one person is a stifling and meddling place to another (which is another reason Americans move a lot). And few Americans want to return to a time when women in the work force faced both formal and informal discrimination.

But it is not an act of nostalgia to assert that crime can, indeed, destroy a neighborhood's capacity to function. It is neither nostalgic nor "backward" for parents to disapprove of some, perhaps many, of the values transmitted by mass culture. Nor can the accusation of nostalgia be used to dismiss the obvious fact that the new division of work between men and women outside the home has not been matched by efforts to ease the impact of all this working on families and children. It is not nostalgia to assert that many of society's voluntary institutions were once sustained by the unpaid, volunteer labor of women, and that we have done little to adjust our civic sector to the just demands of women that they be paid for their work outside the home. And, as Theda Skocpol argues here, professional associations are not the same as more inclusive forms of sociability. Something is lost when social life is organized so heavily around what we do. Professionals, she notes, "see themselves as specialized experts, not as 'trustees of community'."

Thus, the quest for new forms of civil society can be seen as a rational response to social change—not a rebellion against the modern world but a new attempt to deal with modernity's discontents and dislocations. It is an attempt to build the social, communal, ethnic, and neighborhood associations that suit these times, much as the founders of the Boy Scouts, the Knights of Columbus, the Elks, the YMCA, the NAACP, and the Red Cross built comparable (and remarkably durable) organizations a century or so ago.

The authors gathered here, and the many others urging a concern for civil society, are not claiming that civil society is hopelessly broken and that decline and doom await us all. Many (in these essays especially) see effervescence and creativity in the effort to forge new forms of civil society. But they also assert that we are only at the beginning of this quest and that much more social inventiveness is required.

Civil Society and the Flight from Politics

The antigovernment mood feeds the civil society debate in two ways. It leads to demands to reduce government's role and to turn to the nongovernmental sector. But it also suggests a disconnection between the state and the citizen.

Defenders of America's Progressive and New Deal tradition argue that far from being enemies, a healthy national political culture and a healthy civil society are allies. Decay in one sphere can lead to decay in the other. Strong networks of association lead to an enriched sense of representation, greater political efficacy, an enhanced faith in the possibilities of politics.

Perhaps the largest debate among those who share a concern for the heath of civil society is over government's role. That debate appears at many points in these essays, notably in the exchange between Theda Skocpol and William Schambra. They disagree on the role of national institutions and government in promoting a vibrant independent sector. Skocpol asserts flatly that "contrary to the conservative view that federal social policies are harmful to voluntary groups, popularly rooted voluntary associations have often grown up in mutually beneficial relationships with federal policies, including federal 'tax-and-spend' programs." No, says Schambra, vital local communities have been weakened by "the project of building a great national community or family or village. . . . The national community's contempt for and campaign to eradicate local civic institutions is a bedrock of twentieth-century elite discourse." Schambra's view is reinforced here by the argument of Senators Coats and Santorum.

At another point, John DiIulio—one of the country's leading allies of church-based action against poverty and social disintegration—joins the debate. DiIulio warns against the illusion that if government retreats from problem solving, civil society will be miraculously reborn. The requirement, DiIulio argues, is not retreat but a more fruitful collaboration between the institutions of government and those of civil society.

The existence of this debate should be seen as a sign that the civil society idea involves not just anodyne niceness but a serious intellectual and political argument over what social reconstruction requires. In their essay, Senators Coats and Santorum speak candidly about "the beginning of a struggle for political ownership of these powerful themes." My views run much closer to Skocpol's, DiIulio's, and Michael Walzer's than to those of Schambra, Coats, and Santorum. Absent government—absent "public support and backup," as the Reverend Eugene Rivers says—community-based efforts in the nation's poorest neighborhoods will fall short, not for a lack of local commitment and energy but for a lack of resources and power. Nonetheless, the agreement among all these authors that social reconstruction is necessary suggests that the civil society idea is becoming a powerful engine of reform.

In the short run, advocates of civil society might agree that whatever their political differences, democratic systems are in jeopardy if too many citizens feel disconnected not only from this or that political party or politician but also from forms of organizational life that give them an effective voice. They lose hope that they can accomplish what Harry Boyte and Nancy Kari have usefully called "public work," actions designed not simply to help someone in need but also to build up, improve, and solve problems within one's own community or nation.

In the long run, there will be much debate over the question posed long ago by Berger and Neuhaus: what is government's role in promoting civil society? What is the responsibility of companies and employers to organize work so that a citizen, as Theodore Roosevelt put it, "will have time and energy to bear his share in the management of the community?" What are realistic expectations for the voluntary sector? How do companies rooted in an economy that is global and not local relate to and support community works? How does "do good" volunteering support community building by those to whom "good" is presumably being done? This book is offered in the hope of opening such questions rather than closing them.

The Path to Social Reconstruction

The essays that follow try to give shape to the civil society idea and to demonstrate its value in the practical work of rebuilding community. Those by Wolfe and Jean Bethke Elshtain, two pioneers in this argument, discuss civil society's importance directly. Wolfe reflects on developments since the publication of *Whose Keeper?* Elshtain, from whom the title of this essay is borrowed, discusses the importance of civil society to a working democracy. The debate between Theda Skocpol and William Schambra shows how two people devoted to voluntary civil and civic action can disagree sharply about the roots of such engagement.

William Galston and Peter Levine perform a large service by sifting through piles of data and an often acerbic academic argument to give a highly nuanced view of whether or not civil society is on the decline in the United States. Their conclusion, at once sensible and provocative, is that while association building is far from dead, the associations now being built appear less likely than those of the past to foster civic involvement and political participation. "Not all associations promote democratic health in the same way or to the same extent," they note. A corollary finding is that it is a mistake to see the decline in political participation as translating automatically into a decline in social activism and volunteering. In an important contribution to the empirical argument, they suggest that social activism may be increasing as political activism declines.

John DiIulio points to signs of hope in the inner city by throwing light on the immense social capacity of local churches and the successes of faith-based programs that solve problems one person, one soul, at a time. DiIulio asks those concerned about inner-city poverty to consider the huge burden that would be thrown on government if churches, synagogues, and mosques suddenly stopped their good work. Replacing their efforts "would cost literally tens of millions to provide at public expense." DiIulio's essay offers hope that we might have a fruitful rather than a debilitating public debate over the proper relationship between government- and church-based efforts to ease the problems of the poor and to revitalize inner-city neighborhoods. The Reverend Eugene Rivers, whose work is cited by DiIulio and was given wide currency by Joe Klein's *New Yorker* article on his efforts, explains the theory and practice of faith-based community action for the next century. Rivers's moving essay shows how the civil society argument breaks molds in trying to create something new. He is as insistent about the power of faith as he is about the urgency of social justice. He is committed to individual accountability and responsibility, and also to the community's obligation to those trapped in cycles of poverty and dependency.

Bruce Katz tries to solve a puzzle: how is it that although the capacity and competence of community development organizations, local churches, and neighborhood groups has manifestly expanded—exactly as DiIulio says—the social and economic situation of so many inner-city areas has deteriorated? Katz points to a sharp rise in concentrated poverty as the answer, showing how the problems faced by such neighborhoods have multiplied even faster than the capacity to solve them.

The DiIulio and Katz essays taken together point to a highly promising dialogue about both the profound importance of voluntary action rooted in religious and local commitment and the structural limits that the new concentrated poverty may place on such efforts. One might conclude that the activities DiIulio describes are indispensable and worthy of much more support, but that such support will necessarily involve changes in the way metropolitan economies work and in government policies that hurt both inner cities and near suburbs.

Gen. Colin Powell calls for greater commitment from both individuals and the corporate sector to community endeavors, especially helping disadvantaged young Americans. Jane Eisner agrees on the importance of such efforts. But with verve, humor, and common sense, she underscores the extent to which the voluntary sector needs support—and organization.

In all the discussions of the power of volunteerism, few confront such practical issues as: you can't paint a house without paintbrushes or paint. Lurking behind that point is a large and important question: are we tossing large responsibilities to the voluntary sector without thinking first about how to equip volunteers and their organizations with the tools that make for success?

Pam Solo and Gail Pressberg of the Institute for Civil Society, partners with Brookings in our explorations, show success is certainly possible by paying eloquent tribute to those doing the practical work of civil society. David Kuo offers the reflections of a conservative activist who, through a civil society prism, has come to appreciate some of the contributions of liberalism. He suggests how liberals might, in turn, learn a thing or two from conservatives. The tone of his essay points to the possibility that the civil society discussion itself might make the broader political debate a bit more civil.

Alan Ehrenhalt raises uncomfortable questions for liberals and conservatives (and many others, too) and deals explicitly with the problem of nostalgia. He argues that in our longing for a return to the community life of the 1950s, we ignore the extent to which strong communities depend on strong forms of authority against which we have rebelled and continue to rebel. "Authority and community have in fact unraveled together," he says. "We don't want the 1950s back. We want to edit them. We want to keep the safe streets, the friendly grocers, and the milk and cookies, while blotting out the political bosses, the tyrannical headmasters, the inflexible rules, and the lectures on 100% Americanism and the sinfulness of dissent." Ehrenhalt concludes: "Every dream we have about recreating civil society in the absence of authority will turn out to be a pipe dream in the end." Which raises the issue of whether we can create new forms of authority that we regard as less oppressive than the ones we have only recently rejected.

The second section of the book includes responses to the civil society idea from politicians who have been much affected by it. Senators Dan Coats and Rick Santorum, both Republicans, offer the outlines of what might be called compassionate conservatism, an approach rooted in voluntary action but aware that abandoning the welfare state without replacing it would represent a "destructive indifference to human suffering." Former

Senator Bill Bradley offers the reflections of a Democrat who wants government to work, but believes passionately that while public policy "can help facilitate the revitalization of democracy and civil society . . . it cannot create civil society."

The third and final section includes reflections on the civil society idea from two of the country's most powerful social thinkers, Gertrude Himmelfarb and Michael Walzer. They not only speak for divergent political philosophies, but also reach very different conclusions on the subject at hand. Himmelfarb is a decided skeptic about the civil society idea. She suggests that "if people of such diverse views can invoke it so enthusiastically," there may be something terribly flawed or terribly vague about the concept. She argues that the restoration of civil society is less important than the more difficult task of "moral reformation." She worries that what ails us is not the decay of civil society, but the fact that the institutions of civil society *as they now exist* may themselves be "part of the problem rather than the solution." Her essay is a valuable challenge to the spirit that pervades much of this book.

Michael Walzer's essay, with its emphasis on social reconstruction, is a rich tour through the civil society idea and places heavy stress on its value as a vantage point for criticizing the failures of twentieth-century ideologies. Walzer—in contrast to Schambra, Coats, and Santorum—insists on the importance of government, specifically a government rooted in democratic participation. But he also argues that liberals and social democrats need to rediscover the importance of "the world of family, friends, comrades and colleagues, where people are connected to one another and made responsible for each other." His conclusion is as good as one could want for this collection: "Civil society is a project of projects; it requires many organizing strategies and new forms of state action. It requires a new sensitivity for what is local, specific, contingent—and, above all, a new recognition (to paraphrase a famous sentence) that the good life is in the details."

My own view—which, it should be said, is not shared by all the authors in this volume, and is emphatically disputed by some of them—is that the United States is on the verge of a new era of reform similar in spirit to the social rebuilding that took place during the Progressive Era. A time of reform will require three large changes in our national life. First, it will demand a new civility in politics. This is defined not as an avoidance of conflict or difference. It is not simply a call for changing the way we pay for and conduct political campaigns. It is, above all, a demand for a debate at once vigorous, honest, and mutually respectful over what new circumstances require of us. I thank the authors of this volume for debating in that spirit. Second, it will require a new engagement with democratic government and an embrace of the idea that in a democracy, government is not "them" but "us." Democratic government is the realm of self-rule, not an arena of coercion or prescription. Finally, it will entail a rebirth and reconstruction of the communities that constitute civil society, democracy being a community of communities and, as Walzer asserts, a project of projects.

The civil society argument is rooted in a conviction that this generation has the same capacity for social inventiveness demonstrated by the Progressives Teddy Roosevelt led at the beginning of this century and by the socially engaged Americans Alexis de Tocqueville described almost a century earlier. Those who repair to the banner of civil society share a belief that rekindling a spirit of social reconstruction is both essential and a realistic hope.

PART ONE
An Idea and Its Consequences

2

Is Civil Society Obsolete?

Revisiting Predictions of the Decline of Civil Society in *Whose Keeper?*

ALAN WOLFE

REVIVIFIED during the 1980s after a long period of dormancy, the concept of civil society—those forms of communal and associational life that are organized neither by the self-interest of the market nor by the coercive potential of the state—introduced considerable fresh air into both the theory and practice of contemporary societies.

For activists, especially Eastern European dissidents struggling against communist dictatorships, civil society offered a language of volunteerism and freedom. And for social scientists and political theorists everywhere, civil society served as a reminder that even in the modern world there was more to social life than political economy; while no one doubts the power of private companies and public government, families, neighborhoods, voluntary organizations, and spontaneous political movements nonetheless survived and, on occasion, could assume dramatic importance.

No wonder, then, that the idea of civil society went from theoretical and academic conceptualization to fodder for politicians in record time. Left, right, and center found something appealing in the idea. Senator Bill Bradley articulated the theory of civil society to the National Press Club; Senator Dan Coats introduced a series of bills in Congress to promote its recovery; and Gen. Colin Powell spoke the language of civil society at the volunteer summit in Philadelphia. In Pennsylvania and Massachusetts, organizations were founded to promote civil society in American life.

The publication of Robert Putnam's article "Bowling Alone" was greeted by unprecedented media and popular attention to a work of scholarship. While one could—and many did—challenge Putnam's data and interpretations, it was impossible to argue that interest in the idea of civil society was somehow manufactured or ungenuine. Clearly the idea and the national mood worked in tandem.

Too Popular for Its Own Good

Some ideas fail because they never make the light of day. The idea of civil society, many critics charged, failed because it became too popular. One hears this mostly among academics, who rightly, if often intemperately, see it as their mission to question any received or conventional wisdom. For Jean Cohen, who, with Andrew Arato, wrote a massive tome tracing the intellectual history of civil society, the concept that originated out of Hegelian philosophy is inevitably corrupted and cheapened when American politicians try to use it in their speeches. Along similar lines, Adam Seligman argues for "the inadequacy of the idea of civil society as a solution to . . . contemporary impasses." Modern life, Seligman writes, requires ways in which large-scale, impersonal societies can generate trust among strangers, but civil society implies small-scale worlds of personal relationships that are what Seligman calls "presociological" in nature. Civil society, from his perspective, is an anachronism.

While one ought always to welcome criticism of any idea, these kinds of theoretical points strike me as off the mark. It is certainly useful to inquire into the origins of the term civil society and to be reminded of its context in eighteenth-century Scotland or nineteenth-century Germany, but just about all the terms we use today meant something different when they were introduced. When Adam Smith talked about the market, a term he actually used rarely, the systems of exchange he had in mind bear little resemblance to the impersonal, complex, and rule-driven methods of seeking to maximize return that the term has taken on in contemporary microeconomic theory. The same thing applies to a term like civil society. In the writings of Hegel, it may have referred, in Seligman's words, to a realm in which "free, self-determining individuality sets forth its claims for satisfaction of its wants and personal autonomy," but that does not prevent us from using the term today to describe families, churches, and neighborhood associations—so long as we are clear that we are doing so.

Nor is it persuasive to argue, as some critics do, that civil society is a term appropriate to Eastern Europeans trying to carve out free space in a corrupt communist system, but not to Americans thinking about volunteerism. If anything, an understanding of civil society as a realm standing between the market and the state is more relevant to contemporary American experience than it is to the situation in former communist countries. Eastern Europe is experiencing the traumas of the transition to capitalism. Trust, cooperation, and altruism—behaviors generally associated with the virtues of civil society—are not much in evidence; crime, cheating, and rampant suspicion are. Events in that part of the world since 1989 suggest that Eastern European countries will have to pass through some of the more unpleasant dynamics of pure market economies before they will be ready for civil society. Americans, by contrast, have already had their robber barons. Despite our own dispositions toward unfettered capitalism, we have much more strongly developed social institutions capable of cultivating civil society than do Eastern Europeans.

The question is not whether academics and politicians are using the term civil society correctly; it is whether the reality they are trying to capture when they use the term is accurate.

Civil Society in Decline?

A more valuable criticism of the idea of civil society is that writers like Putnam and me, who make the case that civil society has declined, have our facts wrong.

Implicit in this criticism is not just the question of whether soccer leagues are an effective replacement for bowling leagues or whether television is the culprit for declining rates of civic engagement. Rather, moral and political world views clash where the institutions of civil society are presumed to exist. For many feminists, for example, the whole idea that civil society is in decline can be interpreted as part of the backlash against women's entry into the work force, since it was women historically who assumed the burdens of family and communal life.

But it is not just feminists who advance this line of argument. The feminist critique, rather, is shorthand for a defense of modernity against nostalgia. Women's entry into the labor force is just one of many changes in America since the 1950s that can be understood as part of the desire of individuals to have more control over their lives. Others might include greater social and economic mobility, the breakup of neighborhoods organized along lines of racial caste and ethnic homogeneity, and the desires of the young (and the old) for more autonomy. Defending those changes, writers in this tradition argue that we ought to scrutinize carefully any claims that a past golden age was more wholesome than present discontents, if for no other reason than to check the propensity of social critics to romanticize an era which, however communal it might seem in retrospect, gave people less freedom than they have now.

I feel attracted to both sides in this debate. My book, *Whose Keeper? Social Science and Moral Obligation*, published in 1989, was one of the first attempts to take the concept of civil society as it had emerged in Eastern Europe earlier in the decade and apply it to modern Western societies. In that book I spent considerable time comparing the United States, which relies more on the market, with Sweden, Denmark, and Norway, where the state plays a major role. Is there any evidence, I asked, that both kinds of societies, no matter how different in the institutions they use to fulfill moral obligations, are nonetheless similar in neglecting a third realm of social life that is neither economic nor political? My conclusion—based on such indicators of voluntary activity as blood donations, charitable giving, and the treatment of the young and the elderly—was that both did indeed tend to neglect the role of civil society. My book was written from the perspective that civil society would hardly be worth discussing unless it was in danger.

At the same time, I shared the political perspective of the antinostalgia camp. Worried that my book would be interpreted as a call to return to a world of racial caste and gender discrimination, I wrote that a healthy realm of civil society was necessary, not to reject modernity, but to complete its trajectory. Already then, and even more since, I felt a strong distaste for the Jeremiah-like social science practitioner whose description of America in decline seemed to have as much to do with his own distemper as with empirical reality. I hoped that at least parts of *Whose Keeper?* would be proven wrong, as indeed, parts of it were. Scandinavian societies, for one thing, reached the limit of their reliance on the state: Swedes retain their distaste for volunteerism, but they have been forced to cut back the welfare state, while the Danes, who do not like the Swedish cutbacks, have always had more tolerance than the Swedes for private schools or grass-roots organizations. And in America, the very fact that civil society became so popular a term suggested that my predictions of its weakening were premature.

Controversies over the presumed decline of civil society are deep and divisive, but they also serve as a model for how important ideas ought to be discussed. There seems little doubt that some of the more alarmist accounts of civil society's decline, including my own, were exaggerated. Robert Putnam's earlier formulations of the degree to which social capital has been depleted have been effectively criticized by a veritable academic and journalistic industry, but that only testifies to the power of Putnam's way of analyzing the problem, the initially persuasive nature of the data he assembled, and his skill at calling attention to this idea. The social sciences cannot be modeled exactly on the natural sciences, but they do have this one similarity with them: the hypotheses they advance must be subject to as rigorous a process of disconfirmation as possible, after which they ought to be reformulated and reworked to account for alternative data and interpretations. This is exactly what has happened to "Bowling Alone."

Adapting to New Realities

At the same time, there remains an important core of truth in Putnam's argument. When all the data and interpretations are sorted out, my guess is that the story will run something like this: those who worried that civil society was in decline were correct to suggest that something serious was taking place in that realm of social life which—whatever we call it—relies on cooperation, altruism, and intimacy. But those changes can best be understood as qualitative rather than quantitative in nature. It is not the number of organizations to which one belongs that matters. Nor is it whether they require active members or rely mostly on mailing lists. Americans retain their social and civic instincts, but they have little choice but to shape them to the new realities of two-career families, suburban life styles, and rapid career changes. There is little question that the world of civil society at century's end bears little relationship to the images Americans often have of how communal and associational life is supposed to work. There are, however, many open questions about what this new world of civil society looks like and whether it can play the role that important theories of democracy have assigned to civil society in the past.

Less likely to find civil society in neighborhoods, families, and churches, Americans are more likely to find it at the workplace, in cyberspace, and in forms of political participation that are less organized and more sporadic than traditional political parties. Can these newly emerging forms of civil society act as a buffer between the market and the state, protecting Americans from the consequences of selfishness on the one hand and coercive altruism on the other? Will they encourage people to practice political participation, learning through the local and the immediate what it means to be a citizen of the nation and even the world? Are they sufficient to encourage in people a sense of responsibility for both themselves and those with whom they share their society?

We will obviously not have definitive answers to these questions for some time, if ever. Still, I think the outlines of a general answer are already evident. If we listen carefully both to those who worry about civil society's decline and to their critics, we ought to come away impressed by the capacity of Americans to reinvent their worlds. The lament that civil society is in decline too often pays insufficient respect to this perpetual reinvention. It is a testimony to Americans that they constantly tinker with families, neighborhoods, and churches, searching for new forms that provide for both tradition and modernity, freedom, and community. The nostalgia trap is a real one, and we are best off not falling into it.

At the same time, there is no guarantee that new forms of association will satisfy what civil society has often been called on to do. That is why, even as we avoid nostalgia, we also ought to listen to the worrisome tone in accounts of civil society's depletion. The fact that changes in the nature of the family benefit women does not necessarily mean that they benefit children. Organizations devoted to single-issue causes encourage political activism, but not in the same way as organizations more concerned with the public interest. Political campaigning which relies on television can educate voters and turn them out, but does not encourage responsibility in the same way that political parties once did. Churches which recruit new members in ways more similar to therapy than religion have their uses, but encouraging acceptance of the tragic limits to life is not one of them. The more things change, the less they stay the same.

Civil society, in short, is not obsolete; it can never be. Without a realm of associational and communal life independent of the market and the state, we cannot experience the richness of citizenship and the rewards of personal and group responsibility. But one term in the discussion of civil society is, or ought to be, obsolete, and that is the notion of decline. We ought to abolish from our language dealing with social institutions and practices a way of thinking that compares the present with some mythic past—as well as some hopeful future. What we need when we talk about society is not a sense of the worlds we have lost. We need to live in the world we have as best we can. So long as that is the case, civil society will always be around us—and can always be improved.

3

Not a Cure-All

Civil Society Creates Citizens, It Does Not Solve Problems

JEAN BETHKE ELSHTAIN

WHY CIVIL SOCIETY? Why now? That we are debating civil society, its meaning and purpose, is in and of itself fascinating and important. Civil society as a concept has a long and uneven history. For the political philosopher Hegel, it signified a realm of markets and competition and contract whose divisions would be healed over only when the citizen entered the most universal of all ethical realms, that of the state. Civil society, in the Hegelian scheme of things, is a higher realm than that of individuals and families, but definitely lower in the overall picture than the more complete and perfect entity, the state. This European (or, perhaps, more properly "Germanic") way of talking about civil society is not what those claiming the term for contemporary American political debate have in mind, however. For the most part, civil society in our context signifies a sphere of associational life that is, yes, "more" than families and "less" than states, and therein lie precisely its virtues rather than its defects or inadequacies. Americans have always been far more suspicious of the state and concentrations of power at the center than were European state-makers in the heroic era of state creation and legitimation.

By civil society we have in mind the many forms of community and association that dot the landscape of a democratic culture—families (for we often put the family in civil society, although it is lodged there rather clumsily), churches, neighborhood groups, trade unions, self-help movements, volunteer activities of all sorts. Historically, political parties, too, were part of this picture, part of a network that lies outside the formal structure of state power. Observers of American democracy have long recognized the vital importance of civil society thus understood. Some have spoken of "mediating institutions" that lie between the individual and the government or state, locating each of us in a number of little estates, so to speak, which are themselves nested within wider, overlapping frameworks of sustaining and supporting institutions. This densely textured social ecology was—and remains—the ideal. For civil society is a realm that is neither individualist nor collectivist. It partakes of both the "I" and the "we."

Democratic theorists (not all, but most) have issued cautions over the years that America as a democratic culture is perhaps uniquely dependent on vital peripheries, reliant on the vibrancy of political spaces other than or beneath those of the state. These included, of course, town councils and governmental structures of all sorts. But the aim throughout was to forestall concentrations of power at the core or on the top. This is the argument associated with Alexis de Tocqueville in his much-cited classic, *Democracy in America*: only many small-scale civic bodies enable citizens to cultivate democratic virtues and to play an active role in the drama of democracy. Such participation turns on meaningful involvement in some form of community, by which is meant commitments and ties that locate the citizen in bonds of trust, reciprocity, mutuality, competence for the task at hand.

Civil Society's Critics

This all sounds good. Too good to be true, argue some critics, who believe that the current civil society talk is at best a big evasion, at worst a pernicious invitation to triumphant localism. What is being evaded, in the critics' view? The legitimate role of central government, for one thing, for there are tasks only the federal government can, or perhaps should, undertake. This compelling criticism can be addressed and worked out, it seems to me, by noting the ongoing complexities of our federal system. As one example, a spate of Supreme Court decisions this past summer has had, among other things, the effect of opening the door to a revitalization of federalism, even state sovereignty or multiple sovereignties. When I was studying constitutional law in the early 1970s, federalism was considered pretty much a dead letter. Nobody gave a hoot about the Tenth Amendment then. Now it is all the rage. Anthony Lewis, writing in the *New York Times*, dislikes the recent decisions, by "willful members of the Supreme Court" using "strained and rigid readings of the Constitution to strike down New Deal legislation as beyond Federal power." According to Lewis and other representatives of the New Deal type of big government liberalism, the Court is up to nothing less than rolling back history. But for some little government and libertarian conservatives, the Court hasn't gone nearly far enough. As long as the Constitution exists, this movement back and forth is virtually guaranteed.

The Accusation of Nostalgia

The civil society skeptics have other arrows in their quiver, however. The one most commonly shot—rather indiscriminately—skyward is what might be called the Accusation of Nostalgia. I hear it so often that I have an outstanding wager that not a Q-and-A post-lecture or panel discussion will go by without at least one (often rather agitated) member of the audience jumping up to denounce fuzzy-minded evocations of a "Golden Age" and to remind me that there was such a thing as slavery, that awful things happened to Native Americans, that women for many years did not get to vote, and so on. Until recently, I responded with a predictable (and honest) set of caveats. No, this isn't about a Golden Age. Of course, I know many bad things happened and are happening in America. No, I don't think bigots should have a free hand. Of course, the Bill of Rights remains intact, together with the enforcement of subsequent civil rights legislation. This means that the Ku Klux Klan (which comes up frequently, I find, as a peril if there is too much "localism") and others are hauled into court.

But it strikes me increasingly that my shopping list of caveats is rather beside the point. For surely my interlocutors know that I know what they are telling me: that we need a federal government; that we must sometimes override "localism" in favor of something else; that a robust civil society isn't a cure-all and never was. I have decided that the Accusation of Nostalgia is not, after all, a response to my ostensible naiveté or tendency to gloss over past wickedness to skew an argument in my favor—which is what I long figured to be the case. It is about nostalgia. But it isn't mine, or that of other civil society advocates. Rather, it is a yearning on the part of the questioner himself or herself for a world without trade-offs and limits and political opponents with some clout that challenge the presuppositions of what might be called triumphant progressivism. What do I mean? I mean a stubborn refusal to come to grips with the fact that federal-government-centered solutions don't solve all problems or even, more disturbingly, that not all of our problems are fixable. The reality being avoided isn't just that one size doesn't necessarily fit all. It is that many of our troubles are troubles that will plague any mass postindustrial democracy. Civil society isn't so much about problem solving as about citizen and neighbor creating. Then and only then will we work together on other desired ends.

At one point in the not-too-distant past, those who called themselves Progressives embraced the whole Idea of Progress as our version of the Marxist forward march of history to a predetermined goal. Things would get bigger and they would get better. We would become more rational and, as we did so, "local" attachments (often called parochial), commitments to family, religion, and neighborhood (often called backward), would fade. But that hasn't happened. Not only has it not happened, we are now in the midst of a reaffirmation and reassertion of particular identities and commitments, as in the classical Hegelian schema. We know that these can take unpleasant forms. But no civil society thinker wants a world in which there is only civil society—and the whole vast panoply of federal laws and their enforcement has been repealed. Making this clear, however, doesn't satisfy those hurling the charge of nostalgia.

But there is more—more nostalgia from those who accuse civil society thinkers of hankering for the "good old days." It goes like this. Much of 1960s politics was about "Thinking Big" in yet another sense. It was about what were called "movements." The civil rights movement, the antiwar movement, the student movement, the women's movement. Politics was happening, it appeared, only when tens of thousands of people took to the streets, sometimes in the name of nonnegotiable demands. But movement politics is inherently unstable, ephemeral, and geared toward publicity. The movement politics that had the greatest staying power is that which is institutionally tethered, as in the Southern Christian Leadership Conference's mooring in black Baptist congregations. Many of those lodging the Nostalgia Complaint are themselves hankering for a return to big movement politics, it seems. It follows that civil society looks too, well, small; too modest; even, perhaps, too ameliorative.

But you don't have to be Max Weber, with his famous definition of politics as the patient boring of hard boards, to have arrived at the recognition that building and sustaining decent institutions is at the heart of the democratic matter. And movements don't do that—don't build those ties of trust, reciprocity, accountability, mutual self-help over time. No, but institutions, sturdy but resilient institutions of democratic civil society, do. These institutions are, by definition, based on both giving and receiving; on creating a structure of expectations and molding reasonable and decent ways to meet those expectations.

A Job We Can't Give to the Government

Civil society creates spaces for the enactment of human projects, yes, but it also reminds us that this is a world of ties that bind. You cannot have all the good things of democratic life and culture without accountability and duty. Isn't that what the "nostalgia" rebuff is finally all about? We want all sorts of things "solved" once and for all by policymakers and experts and others who will do this job for us. But civil society reminds us of what political philosopher Hannah Arendt called the "elementary problems of human living-together."

In an era—our own—when there is widespread agreement that American democracy is in some trouble, when a mountain of data has been offered up displaying our civic depletion and cynicism, we do well not to yearn for the confident reassurance that government can get things right if we but let it and give it leave to do its job. Government can help or hinder. But it is finally a task for the overlapping, plural associations of civic life in which citizens build and pass on those formative institutions—families, schools, churches, unions, and all the rest, including state and local governments—without which there is no democratic culture and, indeed, nothing for the federal government to either correct or curb or serve.

4

America's Civic Condition
A Glance at the Evidence

WILLIAM A. GALSTON AND PETER LEVINE

THE PUBLICATION of Robert Putnam's "Bowling Alone" in 1995 sparked a vigorous but often murky debate about America's civic condition. Some of the confusion arose from the inconclusiveness of the available data and some from a failure to draw certain basic distinctions.

It is not always recognized that civic health may be measured along several dimensions: participation in electoral politics, political and social trust, voluntary sector activity, and attitudes and conduct bearing on the moral condition of society, to name but a few. No one doubts that many forms of participation in official political institutions and activities have declined in recent decades or that Americans are less inclined to express trust in political leaders—and in one another. It is equally clear that in overwhelming numbers, Americans believe that their society is morally weaker than it once was. Whether they are right to believe this is a different, and more difficult, question. But the fact that they do has contributed to the surprising public salience of what might have remained an abstruse scholarly debate.

When we turn our attention to the voluntary sector, matters become less clear. Here again, some basic distinctions prove useful. Voluntary sector activities include formal organizational membership, volunteering, charitable giving, and informal socializing. Evidence suggests that trends in these areas may be diverging. Moreover, civic trends have not been linear during the past generation. Some declines that began in the 1970s—in aggregate group membership, volunteering, and philanthropy—appear to have halted and even reversed themselves in the late 1980s and early 1990s.

Group Membership

Judged against other industrialized nations, American civil society remains comparatively strong (though its relative standing may have fallen in recent decades). According to the 1990–91 World Values Survey, 82 percent of Americans belong to at least one voluntary association, a rate exceeded only in Iceland, Sweden, and the Netherlands. Furthermore, Americans belong to (and volunteer for) almost all types of groups at above-average rates. Only unions are relatively weak in the United States.

Existing methods for determining and comparing rates of group membership are far from perfect. For example, surveys have not typically asked people how many associations they belong to. Instead, they have asked whether people belong to various types of groups, and answers to these questions have been aggregated to produce a total number of memberships. This aggregate figure is misleading because anyone may belong to several groups of a particular type. Over time, Americans' memberships may have concentrated within certain categories, creating an illusion of decline.

Critics have identified two additional problems with established survey instruments. First, they point out that since strictly comparable poll questions have been asked only since the 1970s, it is hard to know whether aggregate group membership has declined since earlier decades. Second, they argue that existing surveys are unlikely to have captured all recent changes in U.S. associational life—for example, the proliferation of faith-based informal "small groups" that Robert Wuthnow has so painstakingly documented.

Still, there is no evidence that the average rate of membership has increased in the last quarter century. This is a surprise, because in the past rising levels of education have been linked with increased associational activity. It appears that two trends over the past quarter century have roughly counterbalanced each other: the proportion of high school and college graduates in the population has grown larger, but civic participation at every educational level has declined. People with high school diplomas but no college education have become about 32 percent less likely to join any associations, while there has been an increase in the proportion of people who belong to no organizations at all.

Trends among racial and ethnic groups reflect their distinctive history and condition. To take just one example, African Americans have traditionally combined formal political acts, such as registering people to vote, with group membership and protest tactics. Overall, there has been little decline in these forms of civic engagement since the "activist" 1960s, but African Americans have typically shifted their attention from civil rights struggles to quality-of-life issues in local communities. And as Fredrick C. Harris has noted, African Americans without much formal education have, like their white counterparts, largely dropped out of community-oriented activities as well as formal political life.

Another way to break down aggregate measures of civil society is to look at types of organizations. Most categories have seen little change since 1972, when the General Social Survey first asked relevant poll questions. For instance, religious associations, sports leagues, and youth organizations have had stable membership levels. However, millions of people have left labor unions and fraternal societies such as the Elks and Masons, and similar numbers have joined professional associations. Membership in school service groups has substantially increased, perhaps because of recent efforts to link community service and learning. Finally, as Everett C. Ladd has pointed out, there has been a huge shift from mainline Protestant denominations to evangelical churches.

Not All Groups Are Created Equal

These changes may prove significant for the future of democracy in America. Throughout American history, voluntary associations have been valued because they are thought to build civic virtue, foster trust, encourage cooperation, and promote political participation. But on closer inspection, it turns out that not all associations promote democratic health in the same way or to the same extent.

Unions, for instance, are important sources of solidarity among working people. They have core functions that attract members, but they also offer social activities, information, and mutual assistance. They also offer a measure of political power to workers, thereby increasing pluralism and encouraging participation. Members of union households are 8 percent more likely than other people to vote. Though John Brehm and Wendy Rahn have found that union membership is a relatively weak predictor of overall associational membership, Eric Uslaner's research shows that unionized workers join more voluntary organizations and make more charitable contributions than other people do. The dramatic decline in union membership over the past forty years has been exacerbated by factors—automation, international competition, the relocation of factories to nonunion states, and changes in federal labor law enforcement—that do not directly affect other associations.

Fraternal organizations and women's auxiliaries have suffered deep losses in membership since 1974. As Theda Skocpol has demonstrated, these groups traditionally had deep roots in their communities, and they offered men and women of different classes an opportunity to talk and cooperate more or less as equals—something that professional associations, which have grown in recent decades, do not do. The important question is what (if anything) will replace the cross-class local organizations that flourished through most of American history.

Church-affiliated groups are the backbone of civil society in America, involving almost half the population (compared with just 13 percent in the average industrialized democracy). Religious associations offer ways for people to give money, receive aid, hold meetings, recruit members for other associations, and learn about public issues. As Sidney Verba, Kay Lehman Schlozman, and Henry E. Brady have found, they are especially valuable for people with little income or education, who tend not to join other groups. Polls show that membership in such groups correlates with voting, volunteering, charity, and political activity.

Evangelical denominations are no exception. The experience, values, and personal networks that they develop transfer easily to politics. They have little hierarchy, and they demand intense participation from their members. For example, as part of their church activities, Baptists are much more likely to plan meetings and make presentations than are Catholics. The growth of evangelical denominations has introduced many people, especially lower-income people, to the political process and given them powerful tools for mutual aid.

Even as fundamentalist denominations encourage the faithful to rely on one another, however, there is evidence that they promote distrust of outsiders. This practice, ironically, helps voter turnout, because a fervent dislike for others motivates people to vote. The broader point, however, is that increased mutual reliance and trust within groups is not necessarily correlated with increased trust among groups.

Mailing-list associations, from the National Rifle Association to the Children's Defense Fund, have grown since 1970. Members of these groups contribute dues to support professional staff; but they do not donate much time or effort. Presumably, writing a check improves one's skills, knowledge, and interpersonal trust much less than attending a meeting or organizing a grass-roots movement.

But mailing-list organizations must not be stereotyped. The Sierra Club, for instance, has been described as a group whose members merely write checks and read newsletters. But as George Pettinico has noted, in one May weekend, the Los Angeles chapter alone organized thirty-nine events, from classes to camping excursions, that were cooperative and participatory.

The controversy over contemporary national check-writing organizations raises broader historical and political issues about the relationship between top-down and bottom-up activities. Theda Skocpol argues that classic voluntary associations such as the PTA and the American Legion succeeded in creating both effective national lobbying arms and vital chapters or affiliates at the state and local levels, with close communication among the various tiers. It should also be said that even pure mailing-list organizations can be effective political actors, thereby freeing members to perform other civic tasks.

Still, a large shift from grass-roots groups to national membership organizations would be grounds for concern. In general, today's associations offer relatively few opportunities for local leadership and deliberation. The past twenty-five years have seen a marked decline in the share of people who belong to committees and serve as officers of local groups, a trend that parallels declines in such forms of local political activity as attending school board meetings and participating in political parties.

Associational Life and Healthy Democracy

Recent scholarship suggests complex links between associational activities and key political variables such as political participation, social trust, and confidence in government.

Controlling for education and income, members of church groups, neighborhood associations, and sports leagues are especially likely to follow politics and vote—a correlation that supports the hypothesis that political participation is significantly more attractive for individuals who belong to social networks. It's not hard to see why. Making a meaningful decision at the polls requires a big investment of time and attention. Because members of voluntary groups have many opportunities to discuss politics, they can easily acquire information, and they are sometimes persuaded to vote by each other or by local politicians and activists who gravitate to organizations. By urging fellow members to support particular candidates or causes, citizens can multiply their political power.

Most studies find that associational membership is also linked to trust in other people. But researchers differ on the strength of the relationship and on the direction of the causal arrow between the two. A recent poll of Philadelphians by the Pew Research Center for the People and the Press showed no strong direct link between trust and participation in voluntary activities. However, Philadelphians who believed that they could "make a difference" tended to be trusting; they were also especially likely to volunteer.

Interpersonal trust and confidence in government tend to go together. Some research suggests that disenchantment with official institutions is an important cause of wariness toward other people. When political leaders let us down, we draw negative conclusions about human nature in general.

The reverse is presumably true as well: wariness toward other people (stemming from crime, family dysfunction, and other sources) may affect our confidence in politicians.

Yet trust in government has fallen more precipitously than interpersonal trust. Much of the decline took place in 1963–75, an era defined largely by Vietnam and Watergate. And perhaps, to a significant extent, the decline was justified. But there now exists, at least at the extremes, evidence of paranoia rather than healthy distrust. According to a recent study by the University of Virginia's Post-Modernity Project, a fifth of Americans believe that the governing elite is "involved in a conspiracy." Widespread fear of major public institutions not only creates generalized distrust thereby discouraging group membership—but may also cause people to favor exclusive and inward-looking organizations. As noted by Warren E. Miller and J. Merrill Shanks, excessive cynicism about politics and government may well discourage voting and other forms of political participation. A presumption that politicians are unworthy keeps many honorable people out of the field. And a belief in conspiracies prevents citizens from making critical distinctions among leaders, organizations, and ideologies.

A Refuge from Politics?

The evidence now available does not permit firm conclusions about the overall condition of associational life in America. But it does seem that voluntary activities are on balance healthier than are formal political institutions and processes. Indeed, citizens, particularly the youngest, seem to be shifting their preferred civic involvement from official politics to the voluntary sector. If so, the classic Tocquevillian thesis would have to be modified: local civic life, far from acting as a school for wider political involvement, may increasingly serve as a refuge from (and alternative to) it. The consequences for the future of our democracy could be significant.

5

Don't Blame Big Government

America's Voluntary Groups Thrive in a National Network

THEDA SKOCPOL

MANY CONSERVATIVES tend to blame the rise of big government over the course of the twentieth century for the decline of American civil society. Convinced that once upon a time voluntary groups flourished within "self-contained" local communities, they often cite Alexis de Tocqueville in support of the notion that in the early days of the American republic local voluntary groups prospered apart from politics or government above the local level. In reality, however, the great Frenchman's *Democracy in America* repeatedly highlights the ways in which America's nascent electoral democracy promoted all sorts of voluntary associations. And recent research by historians underscores the enduring importance of the U.S. federal government in promoting a vibrant civil society.

Voluntary Groups and National Government

Between the establishment of the Constitution and the 1830s, when Alexis de Tocqueville made his famous visit to our country, the fledgling United States enfranchised most free men and established competitive elections for state and national offices. As Richard Brown has shown, the Revolutionary War and subsequent electoral politics stimulated the formation of new voluntary groups in small villages and towns that otherwise might not have developed such groups. Recently, the historian Richard John has documented that the early republic developed an extraordinarily extensive and administratively efficient national postal system, encompassing even the remotest frontier hamlets. Much bigger than the postal systems of the bureaucratic European monarchies of that time, the U.S. postal system created a network of communication and stagecoach transportation that facilitated commerce, subsidized the dissemination of countless newspapers, stimulated popular political participation, and encouraged the activities of thousands of local and extralocal voluntary associations. One early reform association, the General Union for Promoting the Observance of the Christian Sabbath, took advantage of the mail system to organize a nationwide movement to demand the closing of post offices on Sunday! Temperance crusades and antislavery movements also spread their messages through the mail. In short, a strong and effective national state and a democratic civil society grew up together in early America.

Scholars have documented that the formation of voluntary groups in America came in major bursts. One took place before the Civil War, from the 1820s to the 1840s; others came after the Civil War, from the 1870s through the turn of the twentieth century, and during the 1930s. Waves of voluntary group formation got under way during periods of intense political party mobilization and highly competitive national elections. The waves also coincided with periods of national cultural and political debate—focused before the Civil War on issues of morality and slavery and afterward on responses to industrialization and economic crises.

As part of a Civic Engagement Project at Harvard, my colleagues and I are assembling data on the emergence and growth of large voluntary associations in America. So far we have identified fifty-five "extensive associations"—defined as those that have enrolled 1 percent or more of American adults at any point between 1790 and the present. These groups too were founded in waves that roughly coincided with the more general bursts of activity in voluntary group formation documented by other scholars.

Although the project has just begun developing a detailed "life history" of each of these fifty-five groups, already it is obvious that many groups launched during the 1800s survived and flourished into the twentieth century. In fact, more than four-fifths of all extensive associations ever founded still exist today. As U.S. politics became more nationally focused around the Civil War, World War I, the New Deal, World War II, and the cold war, the voluntary associations did not wither away. On the contrary, many established ones added new local and state units, recruited more individual members, and branched into new activities. For some groups, membership dipped during the Depression when people could not afford to pay dues. Some of those groups never recovered, but others reached further membership peaks during the 1960s and 1970s.

Contrary to the conservative view that federal social policies are harmful to voluntary groups, popularly rooted voluntary associations have often grown up in a mutually beneficial relationship with federal policies, including federal "tax-and-spend" programs. Civil War benefits, for example, stimulated the growth of the Grand Army of the Republic, which in turn promoted and helped to administer federal, state, and local support for veterans and their families. Early twentieth-century local, state, and national policies to help mothers and children were championed by the Women's Christian Temperance Union, the National Congress of Mothers (later the PTA), and the General Federation of Women's Clubs—groups that themselves expanded in part because of encouragement by government. State and federal efforts to support farmers and farm families have been championed and administered by associations such as the Grange and the American Farm Bureau Federation, the latter of which grew into a nationwide federation in conjunction with New Deal farm programs. New Deal social security legislation was originally encouraged by the Fraternal Order of Eagles and the Townsend Movement and has, in turn, stimulated the emergence of more recent local, state, and national associations of the elderly. The GI Bill of 1944 never would have taken the inclusive shape it did, opening up American higher education to hundreds of thousands of less privileged men, had not the American Legion taken the lead in writing generous legislation and encouraging public and congressional support for it. In turn, the GI Bill aided the postwar expansion of the American Legion.

Those who say that America's modern systems of social provision have choked off—or crowded out—voluntary activity in civil society could not be more wrong. America's version of the modern social security state features core programs that give benefits in return for individuals' service to the nation, helping large numbers of middle class and poorer citizens at the same time. This distinctively American social security state has gone hand in hand with locally and nationally vibrant voluntary civic activism. If we dismantle or avoid national social provision in the future, we will harm civil society, not help it.

Local Efforts: Part of Something Bigger

Just as it is a mistake to see the federal government as automatically opposed to a healthy civil society, so too is it wrong to imagine that most American voluntary groups have been self-contained local efforts. Of course, particular groups have come and gone in communities and workplaces. But most local voluntary groups are directly or indirectly linked to parallel efforts across many communities, states, regions, and (often) the entire nation. People in local groups take heart or example from what others linked to them are doing at the same time elsewhere. As the social historian Alexander Hoffman has very aptly put it, "Sustained by both internal and external links, local institutions and organizations may best be understood as branch offices and local chapters—the building blocks of a 'nation of joiners'. . . Americans enlisted in local church groups, fraternal lodges, clubs, and other organizations that belonged to nationwide networks."

Studying just one place at a time, historians have at times mistakenly described local groups as purely idiosyncratic efforts. But systematic data are becoming available to help scholars sorts things out more accurately. Over the past year, for example, Gerald Gamm and Robert Putnam have collected a rich data set counting all the groups listed in directories from more than two dozen cities and towns for each decade between 1840 and 1940. About a third of the groups Gamm and Putnam counted were fraternal or sororal groups—which were central to American social and civic life from the nineteenth century until the 1960s. When the Civic Engagement Project at Harvard took a close look at the fraternal groups mentioned in Gamm and Putnam's local directories, we found that at least three-quarters of the fraternal group titles referred to units within translocal federations. Gamm and Putnam's data set also lists lots of churches, women's clubs, union halls, and service and professional groups—many of which my coresearchers and I believe were linked, during a period of American history that people often imagine to have been a time of localism, into regional or national networks of voluntary associations.

During the entire "modern" era of U.S. voluntarism, from the Civil War to around 1960, the quintessential form of translocal U.S. voluntarism was the federation, linking membership groups in cities and towns into networks with an organizational presence in each of forty-eight to fifty states, and at the same time tying the localities and states into a national organization that ran conventions and disseminated publications. Until recently, most large U.S. voluntary associations have had this three-tiered federal structure, paralleling that of U.S. government: local, state, and national. For U.S. voluntary associations, this federal form has been extraordinarily resilient and flexible. It has allowed local participation and democracy to be combined with group decisionmaking at state and national levels. It has allowed voluntary groups, if they chose, to relate to all levels of U.S. party politics, public administration, and legislative decisionmaking. It has also allowed for pluralism within unity, because local and state groups in particular parts of the country could pursue their own purposes, while at the same time cooperating for other purposes with groups in other places.

A nationwide voluntary association like the American Legion, for example, has deployed the federal form to perfection, as demonstrated by both Richard Jones and William Pencak. Local Legion posts run parades, supervise youth activities, help veterans and their families, and otherwise contribute to, and take vitality from, local communities across America. At the same time, the Legion can and does deliberate about, and then speaks out on, state and national affairs. Like the PTA, the Knights of Columbus, countless fraternal groups, environmental groups, and many other U.S. voluntary federations, the American Legion demonstrates that local community involvement and an intense commitment to national identity have historically gone hand in hand in American democracy. The genius of the most successful and extensive U.S. voluntary efforts has been to make local and state and national commitments complement—rather than oppose—one another.

What Has Gone Wrong Lately?

Recent social shifts in voluntary group activity, however, have made it harder for Americans to band together to get things done—either through or in relationship to government. To be sure, thousands of grass-roots groups and national advocacy groups proliferated between the mid-1960s and the early 1980s—at the same time that the rise of professional groups, trade associations, and think tanks was turning Washington, D.C., into an "imperial" capital, as Kevin Phillips puts it. But there has been a "missing middle" in all this recent associational proliferation—an absence of links from national to local groups. With several notable exceptions, such as the Christian Coalition, few new local-state-national federations have been founded since the 1960s and 1970s. And many of the thirty to forty nationwide voluntary federations that flourished in mid-twentieth-century America have gone into absolute as well as relative membership decline.

Both class and gender transformations have affected U.S. associations. Most large voluntary federations from the 1800s through the 1960s were cross-class, single-gender affairs. Business and professional people joined together with white-collar folks and perhaps with more privileged farmers or craft or industrial workers. But it was predominately men or women, not both together, who formed most of these multipurpose voluntary associations. For much of American history, segregated male and female roles provided broad, shared identities through which huge numbers of Americans could band together across regional and class lines.

Until recently, male military veterans and higher-educated women have been leaders of nationally prestigious voluntary groups. But between 1974 and 1994 better educated women led the way in withdrawing from many types of voluntary federations, while simultaneously increasing their participation in occupationally based groups, such as unions and professional associations. The United States has also developed a very large professional-managerial upper-middle class, full of men (and now women too) who see themselves as specialized experts. Along with business people, today's managers and professionals seem more oriented to giving money to or working with national advocacy organizations than to climbing the local-state-national leadership ladders of traditional voluntary associations.

Better educated Americans, in short, have pulled out of broad community groups in record numbers since the mid-1970s, sometimes leaving behind people with high school educations or less. America's largest cross-class associations have withered. The best educated people are still participating in more groups overall, but not in the same groups as their less-well-educated fellow citizens.

One answer to improving the nation's civic life will turn out, I believe, to lie in encouraging privileged Americans to rejoin—or recreate—the group settings in which they have daily chances to work with a broad cross-section of fellow citizens to address the nation's concerns. Americans need to place a new emphasis on working together, not just on "helping the poor." "Doing with" rather than "doing for" should be our watchword, if we want to revitalize the best traditions of American voluntarism.

6

All Community Is Local
The Key to America's Civic Renewal

WILLIAM A. SCHAMBRA

IN A LEAKY, drafty former VFW hall on Milwaukee's northwest side, Pastor Gerald Saffold is busy rebuilding civil society. Of course, that's not how he would describe what he's doing. He would say that he's bringing souls to Christ—using his gift for music to draw inner-city teens into his "Unity in the Community" Choir, where former gang leaders and drug dealers help him write the songs and choreograph the dances they then perform all over the city.

Nonetheless, here is an unmistakable act of civic renewal, and under the least hospitable circumstances imaginable. Where before there were inner-city gangs of radically alienated, angry teens, there is emerging today a cohesive community, united in common endeavor, mutually developing skills of cooperation, leadership, and citizenship.

Yet, sadly, we as a society do not seem inclined to celebrate this simple gospel choir as a significant civic event. (And this, ironically, in the very face of Robert Putnam's now famous discovery of the link between active choral societies and civic health.) Instead, we seem to be scanning the horizon for larger countrywide movements, for a sweetening of our collective national mood, a restoration of national cohesiveness.

How did we arrive at this preoccupation with national cohesiveness?

That is the story of the idea of national community—the central concept and overriding goal of twentieth-century American progressive liberalism. Early in the twentieth century, our leading political intellectuals—foremost among them Walter Lippmann, Herbert Croly, and John Dewey—concluded that the forces of modernity were rapidly and irretrievably eroding the traditional institutions of civil society. Within such institutions—small towns, churches, neighborhoods, and ethnic and religious groups—Americans had traditionally governed themselves, established and preserved their own vigorous moral and religious cultures, cared for their most vulnerable, and met the human yearning for community.

But now, the progressives warned, the boundaries of these "island communities" had been hopelessly ruptured by modern technologies—the railroad, telegraph, telephone, the high-speed press, the corporation. These same technologies, however, made possible a new and dramatically improved form of community—the great national community. Elaborate communications and transportation networks would pull the nation together even as they pulled the village apart. And the emerging social sciences would tame the disintegrative sociological and psychological effects of modernity, once enough experts in government, business, and the nonprofit sector were trained in them and organized into the imposing bureaucracies that would now "scientifically manage" all human affairs.

To bring comprehensive order to all these forces, Theodore Roosevelt proclaimed in 1912, we now required a far more powerful central government. At the apex of this new federal apparatus, a dynamic, articulate president would mount the "bully pulpit" and summon the American people out of modernity's fragmented individualism into unified, high-minded national endeavor. The stirring rhetoric of national crisis and war would provide the metaphors needed to make the American people sense, as the late Robert Nisbet put it, "their mystic national oneness."

This century's political life has been dominated by the project of building a great national community or family or village, peaking in Lyndon Johnson's effort to "turn unity of interest into unity of purpose, and unity of goals into unity in the Great Society." We have been exhorted by Franklin Roosevelt to unite in the face of the Great Depression "as a trained and loyal army willing to sacrifice for the good of a common discipline"; by

John F. Kennedy to "ask not what our country can do for us, but what we can do for our country"; by Lyndon Johnson to wage a "war on poverty." Through these galvanizing metaphors of war and crisis, the presidency sought to fulfill its primary purpose, which is, as Walter Mondale put it in 1984, to "make us a community and keep us a community."

As noble as this ideal may seem—as necessary as national unity may be in the face of genuine emergencies or war—progressivism's national community has proven in political practice to be this century's greatest disappointment. Though it has drained the strength and moral authority from local community institutions, it has failed to build the promised national substitute.

The national community's contempt for and campaign to eradicate local civic institutions is a bedrock of twentieth-century elite discourse. Local institutions, it is said, are notoriously and hopelessly backward, partial, parochial, reactionary, and riddled with irrational myths and prejudices. They cling stubbornly to obscure and retrograde notions of traditional morality and religious faith, rather than bowing sensibly to the authority of scientifically credentialed professionals and experts, who alone can exploit the potential of modernity.

How many campus-bred intellectual doctrines, how many short stories and novels, how many Hollywood movies and television shows, have reveled in this contrast between shabby, small-minded, local prejudices and a sophisticated, expansive attachment to national ideals? Given the unremitting hostility of America's elites throughout this century, is it any wonder that local civic institutions might today find themselves in an uphill struggle for survival?

That the idea of national community has failed to deliver on its central promise—to reestablish at the level of the nation as a whole the sense of belonging, purpose, and self-governance that local institutions once provided—is now commonly considered a conservative argument. But the insight by no means originated on the right. Indeed, as Nisbet pointed out, conservatism wasted much of this century futilely extolling the virtues of rugged individualism and the untrammeled marketplace in the face of America's manifest yearning for some form of community.

Rather, the bankruptcy of the idea of national community was the central insight of the New Left of the 1960s and of Saul Alinsky's community organizers, before and since. They initially and correctly observed that the Great Society had not in fact delivered the great community, but rather only the cold, distant, alienated bureaucracies of "corporate liberalism." The vast, impersonal institutions of business and government, they argued, simply could not provide the self-governance and community of "participatory democracy" for which the human spirit yearned.

Conservatism has indeed more recently taken up this general theme, though not at all in the spirit of the 1960s. To be sure, participatory democracy is essential for human happiness, conservatism maintains, but the peculiarly American way of achieving it has always been through dutiful citizenship within traditional, local institutions like the church, neighborhood, and voluntary association. That Republican presidents were swept into office throughout the past three decades on this theme proved its power; that a Democratic president recently won reelection on this same theme marks its moment of supreme triumph.

But the subtle allure of the national community idea is still very much evident today and tends to undermine even the most sincere efforts to restore civic institutions. Our national ambivalence is nicely reflected in Hillary Rodham Clinton's recent *It Takes a Village.*

Ms. Clinton readily concedes what progressivism had denied for much of this century—that strong families, neighborhoods, and churches, far from being merely nurseries of reaction and bigotry, are essential to the physical, psychological, and moral well-being of children. That stated, however, she quickly reverts to themes more congenial to the project of national community: that such traditional local institutions have been hopelessly undercut by technology; that we therefore must now rely heavily on the advice and assistance of trained professionals and experts; and that we should consider a variety of new government institutions to ensure that all families are able to secure such advice and assistance. The small, real-life village quickly yields to the metaphorical national village.

Likewise, discussions of revitalizing civil institutions tend to focus on a limited range of major national nonprofits like the PTA or the Red Cross, which are by no means incompatible with the idea of national community. Though these organizations may have local chapters, they often look to the

Washington office for marching orders, receive federal funding, press policy agendas on the federal government, and have gradually displaced the leadership of local amateurs and volunteers with centralized bureaucracies of scientifically trained experts and professionals. Such "acceptable" civic institutions can even be counted on to go before congressional committees and testify that they would languish, rather than prosper, were government's benevolent presence to be diminished any further.

It is now permissible—indeed, fashionable—to fret about the health of such organizations, because of course they do not at all undermine, but rather tend to reinforce, the upward political tug of the national community idea. It is seldom noted that perhaps their health is imperiled precisely because they have exchanged their historic roots in the neighborhood for invitations to cocktails in the salons of our political and cultural elites. Perhaps their predicament is not a proper gauge of the well-being of American civil society after all.

These examples suggest that while the moral authority of the idea of national community has been seriously eroded over the past several decades, it has nonetheless left in its wake towering bureaucracies of elites and experts—not only within government, but in the nonprofit sector as well—who have powerful vested interests in the renationalization of the idea of community. As they argue eloquently and forcefully, "civic renewal" means restoring the deference and respect owed by a mystifyingly ungrateful public to the major institutions working on behalf of the noble idea of national community.

I would suggest, on the contrary, that it's time to look in the opposite direction, away from the exhausted ideal of national community and toward the small but vigorous civic community that Pastor Saffold is building on Milwaukee's northwest side. As Bob Woodson has argued so forcefully over the years, there are in fact hundreds of Saffolds in America's inner cities, working quietly, successfully, and without public acclaim to battle drug abuse, educate children, reclaim teens from gangs, and rebuild neighborhood economies—in other words, to accomplish as small, local civic institutions what government bureaucracies never could.

Throughout our nation faith-based grass-roots leaders are managing—at a time and in places where the bureaucracies of business and government and the mainstream nonprofits have thrown up their hands and fled—to resurrect the institutions and principles of civil society. They are civil society's trauma specialists—and the true experts on civic renewal.

Yet to our elites, these grass-roots initiatives are invisible, or if visible, dismissed as charismatic exceptions or inspiring but isolated anecdotes. After all, they're not docile subsidiaries of the larger, "acceptable" nonprofits, but rather scrappy, scruffy, fiercely independent local initiatives, too busy working with the poor to join coalitions against poverty. They are not staffed by credentialed bureaucrats, but by volunteers whose chief credential may be that they themselves have only recently overcome the daunting circumstances of the inner city. They place little faith in the rehabilitative powers of the social sciences, but witness every day the fruits of their faith in the transformative power of God.

The disdain of elites notwithstanding, we should heed the wisdom of these grass-roots leaders who have, against heavy odds, accomplished the civic revival that we wish for all our communities. We should appreciate them, honor them, celebrate them. We should also highlight the ways in which private and public resources can be redirected to those who have already accomplished so much with virtually no outside help at all. Here the federal government should have a role too—not as grand builder of national community, but as humble servant to the genuine community builders within our neighborhoods.

When the VFW decided a while back to close its hall on Milwaukee's northwest side, no doubt that retreat of a major national nonprofit was carefully toted up as one more loss on Putnam's gloomy balance sheet of civil society. When Gerald Saffold once again filled the old hall with joyous music, no doubt that vigorous advance of civic renewal went unrecorded. It is past time to direct our gaze away from the failed project of national community and focus once again on the churches, voluntary associations, and grass-roots groups that are rebuilding America's civil society one family, one block, one neighborhood at a time.

7

The Lord's Work

The Church and Civil Society

JOHN J. DiIULIO JR.

IN THE LATE 1980s and early 1990s, a group of black inner-city ministers in Boston organized themselves around a plan for cutting juvenile violence, reclaiming parks and sidewalks, educating at-risk children, promoting local economic development, strengthening families, and resurrecting the civil life of their jobless drug-and-crime-infested neighborhoods. The plan, which included everything from summer recreation and literacy training programs to faith-based one-on-one drug treatment and neighborhood patrols, was not hatched by academic experts, funded by major foundations, praised by leading pundits, or guided by government agencies. Rather, it was based on what the ministers and their small but dedicated cadre of young adult volunteers had learned up close and personal after years spent living, working, and walking—every day—among the poorest of the urban poor and their children.

Good News

In fact, the effort was forged from what the clergy and church volunteers had learned from the local drug kingpins whom they were struggling to save from addiction, violence, jail, death—and damnation. The Reverend Eugene F. Rivers III, the Pentecostal minister of the Azusa Christian Community church who spearheaded the effort and whose own humble inner-city row house was twice sprayed with bullets, recalls one searing insight: "Nearing exhaustion, we asked this one major local dealer, 'Man, why did we lose you? Why are we losing other kids now?' He stares us in the eye and says, 'I'm there, you're not. When the kids go to school, I'm there, you're not. When the boy goes for a loaf of bread or wants a pair of sneakers or just somebody older to talk to or feel safe and strong around, I'm there, you're not. I'm there, you're not; I win, you lose.'"

Helped from the start by Boston's Catholic Church and several local synagogues, the black inner-city ministers' community-saving effort won wider support in 1992 after a group of gang members burst in on the funeral service of a boy killed in a drive-by shooting and stabbed another child in front of the shocked congregation. In the words of the Reverend Jeffrey Brown, a Baptist pastor who has worked closely with Rivers, "That horrible event was the proverbial wake-up call, not only to other local churches and people of the faith, but to the political and other powers that be."

Soon the local press and lots of state and local politicians began to acknowledge the ministers' work. In turn, local police and probation officials who had been highly dubious of partnering with the preachers started working hand-in-hand with the clergy on a wide variety of antigang policing, juvenile probation monitoring, and crime prevention initiatives.

One much-publicized result: Boston has not had a gun-related youth homicide since July 1995, and everyone from the city's mayor to its in-the-trenches probation officers acknowledges that it could not and would not have happened without Rivers, Brown, and the other clergy and church volunteers. "With the churches," one veteran Boston police officer recently told a group of Philadelphia clergy, "with cooperation, we can turn our neighborhoods around. Without them, without cooperation, we can't."

Beyond Boston

Rivers and Brown, together with the Reverend Kevin Cosby of Louisville, Kentucky, and the Reverend Harold Dean Trulear of Philadelphia, have formed a national "leadership foundation" that seeks to bolster ongoing faith-based inner-city youth and community development activities and mobilize at least 1,000 inner-city churches around a Boston-style effort in the forty most blighted neighborhoods of the nation's twenty-five largest cities, all by the year 2006. In May, the Institute for Civil Society, a new New England–based philanthropy, gave the effort a three-year $750,000 seed grant. "In Louisville," says Cosby, "we've held organizing meetings and had 2,500 people show up, ready to go." "Likewise," reports Trulear, "more than a thousand churches in metropolitan New York alone are doing some type of youth and community outreach ministry, and several new and revitalized networks of churches are doing the same in metropolitan Philadelphia."

Already, Rivers and Brown have taken part in what appear to be promising initial mobilization efforts in over a half-dozen cities from Chicago to Tampa. Meanwhile, over the past year or so, their efforts have attracted favorable interest from national journalists, corporate leaders, politicians, academics, and others, including influential Boston area individuals and institutions that, as Rivers and Brown emphasize to the clergy who are beginning to organize in other cities, "didn't want to be connected with the churches, didn't 'do God,' didn't return our phone calls, and literally wouldn't give us the time of day a few years ago even though we were in their own inner-city backyards."

That's the good news. Now, however, for the bad—or, more precisely, the complicating—news, first with respect to the Boston story and next with respect to the overarching reality that not even an army of well-led, well-supported churches and faith-based programs could save the nation's most severely at-risk children, revitalize blighted neighborhoods, and resurrect the civil society of inner-city America without the active human and financial support of suburban churches, secular civil institutions, profit-making corporations, and, last but not least, government at all levels.

Back to Boston. For all the attention, praise, and publicity, Rivers, Brown, and the local church volunteers there are still wanting for new volunteers and still lacking in financial support. Explains Eva Thorne, a Ph.D. candidate in political science at M.I.T. who, together with other young black professionals, has worked with the Boston ministers for nearly a decade and who is preparing a church-anchored, multimillion dollar redevelopment plan for Dorchester:

"Everybody celebrates the success and says 'amen,' but most people, especially most educated people, remain deeply conflicted about working on social and economic problems with and through churches. For some, it's an underlying suspicion that churched folks are stupid, and a more generalized hostility to religion and all things religious. For others, it's more a church-state thing, which mediates their thinking even where government isn't at issue in what we're trying to do. For many, it's even deeper than that. You know, 'I'm not going out there with those drug addicts and violent kids! I'm not getting sweaty and giving up my free time. And I'm not giving money or other help to anyone who's fool enough to do it.' So there are those who are weirded out by your walk-among-the-poor religious motivation, those for whom it's too real and too strong. But, then, blocking you on the opposite side are those who think your religious motivation is, in effect, too weak or false, the 'all inner-city preachers are pimps with collars' school. It's very frustrating."

As Rivers, Brown, and their street-smart minions reflect on the "24-7-365, fall asleep in our clothes" efforts it took to get a faith-friendly handle on local youth gangs and reduce juvenile gunplay in their neighborhoods, they feel daunted by the prospect of a dramatic increase in poor, young, fatherless, jobless black males. Local researchers project that the number of black male residents of the city between the ages of fourteen and twenty-four will grow to over 30,000 by 2005, roughly a threefold increase over the number residing there in 1995. "Many of these children," warns Rivers, "are the four- to fourteen-year-olds running around at night on our streets without any adult care or guidance. We're trying to reach their mothers, reconnect them with fathers or father figures, and take them on in a holistic way. But their social force is growing at least as fast as ours, coming up as they are the first children born in the wake of the crack cocaine crisis and the welfare cutoffs."

In response, the ministers are redoubling their work on an ambitious pilot project, called Operation 2006, which seeks to involve clergy and church volunteers in the lives of every one of the city's most severely at-risk youngsters, providing counseling and community service employment for their parents or legal guardians, and offering the children everything from after-school safe havens and decent meals to adult-supervised recreation programs and community-based juvenile probation ombudsmen. "We hope churches in Philadelphia and other cities," remarks Trulear, "will work to do the same, but our churches cannot even begin to do it alone."

No, they can't.

Faith Factors

It's true that most of the best recent empirical research suggests that inner-city churches, especially black congregations, are leveraging several times their weight in community service. For example, a 1990 study of more than 2,100 urban black congregations found that about 70 percent sponsored or participated directly in community outreach activities—staffing day-care facilities, offering substance-abuse prevention programs, administering food banks, building shelters, and more. A 1994 compendium of research on the subject referenced scores of studies showing that most urban black churches are involved in community efforts ranging from housing and health services to preschools and elementary education.

Eighty-five percent of black churches in Atlanta, according to one study, are engaged in some type of outreach program beyond religious services to their congregations. And a forthcoming, in-depth, multicity survey commissioned by Partners for Sacred Places, a Philadelphia-based nonprofit group interested mainly in the historic preservation of older urban churches, synagogues, and temples, will provide the most conclusive evidence yet that big-city churches anchor an incredible array of youth and community development efforts—efforts that would cost literally tens of millions to provide at public expense.

But as economists Linda Loury and Glenn Loury recently intimated, we remain a long way from a definitive body of research evidence on the actual extent and the efficacy of church-anchored and faith-based social programs.

Most of the preliminary evidence is indeed encouraging, including studies showing that churched young black urban males have brighter life prospects (lower rates of crime, drugs, and joblessness) than otherwise comparable unchurched youth; that faith-based programs in prisons have measurable rehabilitative effects; and more.

Still, the "faith factor" literature remains in its infancy, and, even with the recent surge of interest in the topic among leading social scientists and policy analysts, it will be some time before we can identify the conditions, if any, under which given types of church-centered programs work, or specify how, if at all, faith-based efforts can be taken to scale in ways that cut crime, reduce poverty, banish illiteracy, or yield other positive, predictable, and desirable social consequences.

Church Anchors

As this research goes forward and as ministers like Rivers rally support to their noble cause, it will be crucial for all concerned to understand inner-city churches as part of what Lester Salamon terms "the civil society sector."

In the January/February issue of *Society*, Salamon challenged the conventional view of civil society as a diverse set of nonmarket, nongovernmental institutions—"savings associations, church choirs, sports clubs, charities, and philanthropic foundations"—whose unique mission is to create "networks of civic engagement that produce and enforce communal values and notions of trust so necessary for cooperation and civil life." This view, he argued, "overlooks the extent to which the 'civil society sector' relies on other sectors to survive."

Drawing an impressive array of data on the civil society sector in the United States and other democracies, Salamon puts a huge empirical question mark over the idea that as "the state expands, it therefore renders voluntary organizations functionally irrelevant, thereby contributing to the decline and undermining the spirit of community which they sustain." Instead of the "zero sum, conflictual image of the relationship between the civil society sector and the state," the data he examined painted a more complicated picture of "three more or less distinct sectors—government, business, and nonprofit—that nevertheless find ways to work together in responding to public needs." So conceived, he reasoned, "the term 'civil society' would not apply to a particular sector, but to a relationship among the sectors, one in which a high level of cooperation and mutual support prevailed."

Some conservative champions of faith-based efforts seem to suppose that it is only liberal welfare state apologists and spokespersons for big, largely government-funded religious charities who are cautioning that churches and other civil institutions cannot fill the financial and social services gaps left by government withdrawal from low-income cash and in-kind assistance for the poor. They're as wrong as they are wrongheaded.

As former Secretary of Education William J. Bennett and Senator Daniel Coats, Republican of Indiana, argued publicly in 1995, "the retreat of government does not always, at least not immediately, result in the rebirth of civil society." Or, in Rivers's words, "Without public support and back-up, financial and logistical, there's no way churches or other community folk can turn the tide. But if we learn how to work together, then there's no limit to what can be accomplished before it's too late."

Spiritual Capital

Amen. It is also important to think critically about faith communities in relation to broader debates about the state of civil society and to ask how much of urban America's ostensibly dwindling stock of social capital is, as it were, "spiritual capital."

In several articles published in the mid-1990s, beginning with the much-noted "Bowling Alone," political scientist Robert Putnam highlighted evidence of "a broad and continuing erosion of civic engagement that began a quarter century ago." Fewer and fewer Americans, he argued, were voting, joining the PTA, going to church, or participating in other civic associations and group activities.

Putnam's thesis about the decline of social capital has been criticized on many different grounds, and the scholarly scrap over civil society is far from over. One thing, however, is indisputable. While more Americans are now bowling alone, scores of millions of Americans are still praying together and volunteering through their churches.

Outstanding survey research produced by George Gallup Jr. plainly documents that most Americans believe in God, belong to a church or synagogue, and acknowledge that religion is very important in their lives. Moreover, more than 60 percent of all Americans, and more than 80 percent of black Americans, believe that religion can answer all or most social problems.

Churches are the country's single biggest source of volunteers, way ahead of workplaces, schools or colleges, fraternal groups, and other civil institutions. As Gallup has summarized the evidence, "Churches and other religious bodies are the major supporters of voluntary services for neighborhoods and communities. Members of a church or synagogue . . . tend to be much more involved in charitable activity, particularly through organized groups, than nonmembers. Almost half of the church members did unpaid volunteer work in a given year, compared to only a third of nonmembers."

Charitable Choice

Finally, it is vital to remain focused on how churched volunteers and the rest of the civil society sector respond to today's ever more highly devolved federal welfare regime.

Section 104 of the Personal Responsibility and Work Opportunity Reconciliation Act of 1996 (a.k.a. the welfare law) encourages states to engage faith-based organizations as providers of welfare services funded by Washington—job search programs, maternity homes for expectant unmarried minors, drug-treatment programs, and much more. Under this so-called charitable choice provision, religious providers that accept government funds have the right to maintain their religious character—displaying religious art, using religious criteria in personnel decisions, and limiting the range of government audits by placing federal funds into separate budgets.

At this point, it remains unclear how, whether, or to what extent churches will take advantage of the charitable choice provision, and, if so, with what consequences. In fact, we may never know. Even before the welfare law was enacted, scores of national and state research projects were planned to monitor the impact of welfare devolution. But almost no attention is being paid to the implementation of the charitable choice provision.

In a 1995 lecture, Nobel economist Robert W. Fogel argued that the United States is now in the midst of a "Fourth Great Awakening," a "new religious revival fueled by a revulsion with the corruptions of contemporary society," and effecting a "political realignment"evidenced by the legislative handiwork of the Republican-led 104th Congress.

A most sweeping and provocative big-think thesis, but one best pondered by preachers, politicians, pundits, public administrators, and policy analysts who first take care to see whether anyone greatly awakens to charitable choice, and, if so, how and with what results.

8

High-Octane Faith and Civil Society

EUGENE F. RIVERS III

IN MANY OF OUR inner-city neighborhoods, the black churches are the only structures still standing. I mean that both literally and metaphorically. The African-American churches of urban America have provided practically the only sanctuary in these violent, unpredictable places, and even they have not been immune to the degradation of dark, urban life. As a son of the high-octane wing of the black church—we're full of fire, but on occasion we lack the light to illuminate our own way—I've learned a few lessons over the years about the connections that make neighborhoods either productive communities or traps from which many never escape. I've learned, too, about my own faith and the restorative power of belief. I've also learned that a welfare program can provide nothing to equal the power of faith in reclaiming lives from the clutches of poverty and despair.

The Azusa Christian Community in Boston, of which I am now pastor, began as a student group at Harvard University during the early 1980s when we were confronted by the growing class polarization and inequality in the black community. Inspired by Catholic social teaching to live in material and spiritual solidarity with the poor, we moved our church into a low-income neighborhood, one we later discovered was one of the most violent in Boston. Dorchester, particularly the Four Corners area within it, was the kind of place where people brand you a fool for venturing out at night. Other than the liquor stores, there were no businesses; parks were for crack dealers, not children. Poverty, drugs, hopelessness were the victors in Dorchester. The neighborhood had been abandoned by everybody who had someplace else to go—even the black churches had largely turned their backs on the young black men who roamed the streets, predators amongst their own people. Dorchester reminded us of God's warning that if you do not attend to the needs of the children, you will be cursed. The sins of the parents will be visited upon the second and third generations. Certainly we were then—and are still now—reaping the whirlwind of not teaching our children the right lessons.

So we set out to change that, to rescue a forsaken people. The question was, how? How do we rescue the young black men and women from the streets and help a dying—perhaps already dead—neighborhood to be reborn? At first we thought that mere acts of mercy would be enough. We were activists after all, who had grown up with the civil rights movement, who had grown to believe that a helping hand was all you needed. We were accustomed to talking about rights and justice, and we hoped that this message would resonate with these young people. We found out quickly, however, that these young black men and women needed a whole lot more than talk about rights.

A conversation with a young heroin dealer convinced us that we were going about things the wrong way. In essence, he asked us why, if we did all these works in God's name, did we never talk about God? Why, if we were following Jesus' example, did we never mention Jesus by name? All this time we had been doing our good works, we were worried about being offensively religious. We didn't want folks to know too much about our faith, and we hoped to win them over by substituting an emphasis on justice for a call to faith. We realized the hard way, as the people of Dorchester had, that secular solutions could never work in these forgotten pockets of despair. We realized that therapeutic institutions such as government, foundations, public schools, and the whole panoply of non-faith-centered self-help outfits could not speak to the depth of psychic and moral decay that plagued our inner cities. The black leadership of the civil rights era had no answers for the generation born into chaotic, broken families, who would be lured by the culture of violence to gangs and drugs and destruction. The language of civil rights was ineffectual in battling contemporary moral issues. The language that worked was the familiar, transformative language of the Gospel. We found that only by offering to feed the souls of these children could we turn a generation around and bring hope back to our communities.

It took a tragic though seminal event to gather the black churches of the community to work against the blight of drugs and violence. In May 1992, gang members burst into the funeral of a young man who had fallen victim to the streets. In the presence of the mourners, the gang killed one of those in attendance. That brazen act told us we had to do more. Now. That young man's death galvanized us, and soon the Ten Point Coalition was reaching out to at-risk youth. Our mission was to pair the holy and the secular, to do whatever it took to save our kids. The black churches worked hand-in-hand with the schools, courts, police, and social service agencies. We called on anyone and everyone who had the means to help our children. We formed programs for teens, neighborhood watches, and patrols. Most importantly, we walked the streets and preached the gospel, no longer whispering the word of God but boldly declaring our faith. We established ourselves in the neighborhood, standing on the same street corners where the drug dealers once stood. We tracked down the thieves, dealers, and gangs. We tried to give people a chance but if they wouldn't take it, we staked our claim and ran them out of our neighborhood.

The results of our efforts were immediate. In one year alone, 1995–96, the murder rate in Boston dropped 39 percent. That happened not just because we were out walking around at night, but because we were offering something better. We were offering an alternative to violence and self-hatred, and the kids responded. We knew that the presence of the Divine in a child's life makes that child feel differently about himself because it is the Divine that establishes the sacredness of the human experience.

During our struggle to reclaim a whole generation, we said what a lot of left-wing activists didn't want to hear. We told the people that the government couldn't help them. We knew that the solutions had to be worked out in the streets. We told people then—and still tell them—that if you really understand the suffering through which these people are now struggling, you will understand that we desperately need a body of social thought that is rooted in a clearly understood theological affirmation. This must be the basis for policy formation. Each day 1,118 black teenagers are victims of violent crime; 1,451 black children are arrested; 907 black teenage girls get pregnant. A generation of black males is drowning in its own blood. And things are likely to get much worse. Today, some forty years after the beginning of the civil rights movement, younger black Americans are growing up unqualified, even for slavery. The result is a state of civil war, with children in violent revolt against the failed secular and religious leadership of the black community.

Consider some dimensions of this failure. A black boy has a 1-in-3,700 chance of getting a Ph.D. in mathematics, engineering, or physical sciences; a 1-in-766 chance of becoming a lawyer; a 1-in-395 chance of becoming a physician; and a 1-in-195 chance of becoming a teacher.

But his chances are 1 in 2 of never attending college, even if he graduates from high school; 1 in 9 of using cocaine; 1 in 12 of having gonorrhea; and 1 in 20 of being in prison while in his 20s. Only the details are different for his sisters. Yet the most profound dimension of the crisis is not material or spiritual—not political in any formal sense. It is the death of hope.

The pastors and congregants who've helped restore the inner-city black communities in Boston have undoubtedly accomplished great things. The churches have realized their own power to effect a change. They have begun turning things around and getting kids going in a positive direction, but the work remains daunting. Everyone knows that. The sense of safety, peace, and hope that has been restored on the streets of Boston remains fragile. Without solid public backing, particularly without financial help to these public-private partnerships, this hard-won peace will prove nothing more than a lull in the fighting, a momentary cease-fire in the ongoing war that we have been losing to the detriment of every citizen, black and white, for decades.

All this good work should get those people who forge social, crime, and drug policy thinking. They should be asking—as I have asked—this question: if these people in Dorchester have accomplished this miracle with next to no resources, what could they do if they had the means? By bringing together the best of secular and faith-based programs, we can build communities where hope is a permanent legacy, where every succeeding generation builds on the dreams and hard work of the one before. One hundred years ago, in the shadow of slavery, black people were full of faith and hope rooted in the Christian understanding of reality. In the face of what seemed insurmountable obstacles, of pogroms and systematic discrimination, these people prevailed over tragedies and decline. Through the eyes of faith, they can see the unimaginable. But when faith and hope have died . . . well, we've seen what happens then. History and identity themselves are divested of meaning, and life for millions of young people is transformed in a spectacle of nihilism and decay.

We are in a position to transform people's understanding of personal commitments, to help them understand that freedom is not free. Only as the poor are empowered to do for themselves as a result of the power of God in their lives will they be able to make that change. By 2005, the number of at-risk black and brown youths between the ages of fifteen and nineteen will increase 27 percent. The challenge is before us. Never before have the communities of faith been in a better position to articulate reconciliation. To rebuild lives and communities, why not use what we already know works? It is not social policy that fuels the fires of our souls, but God's word.

9

Give Community Institutions A Fighting Chance

BRUCE KATZ

OVER THE PAST several decades, American cities have witnessed an explosive growth in the capacity and expertise of community development corporations, church- and community-based organizations, and community lending institutions. These groups—the front lines of the national discussion over "civil society," "community empowerment," and "social capital"—have made discernible progress in some of the most distressed communities in the country. They have produced and financed affordable homes and, to a lesser extent, invested in commercial enterprises and engaged in anticrime, child care, job training, health care, and other activities.

Most remarkably, this progress has been made in the face of powerful economic and demographic forces—the rise in concentrated urban poverty and the ongoing exodus of middle class families and low-skilled jobs to the metropolitan outskirts—that have destabilized the cities and neighborhoods in which community institutions operate. Left unchecked, these forces can eviscerate the contributions of community-based groups.

The larger trends shaping America's inner-city neighborhoods are not, contrary to conventional wisdom, the exclusive work of invisible market and consumer forces. They are also the result of government subsidies and policies. To ensure the continued success of community-based development groups, federal policies and private sector actors must do more than seed, reward, and enhance their efforts. They must help shape an economic context in which those efforts can succeed.

The Rise in Concentrated Urban Poverty

America's most disturbing demographic trend—rarely discussed during the welfare debate—has been the explosive growth in concentrated poverty, particularly minority poverty, in urban communities. According to the Clinton administration's 1997 "State of the Cities" report, the poverty rate in cities rose almost 50 percent, from 14.2 percent in 1970 to 20.6 percent in 1995.

Trends in inner-city neighborhoods have been even worse. According to Harvard's Paul Jargowsky, the number of people living in high-poverty neighborhoods just about doubled between 1970 and 1990. Some 8 million people, nearly a third of them children, now live in neighborhoods where more than 40 percent of residents are poor.

These neighborhoods are especially likely to house minorities. Between 1970 and 1990, the number of African Americans living in high-poverty areas climbed from 2.4 million to 4.2 million. An incredible one-third of all African-American poor now live in such communities. Three out of four poor African Americans live in neighborhoods where more than 20 percent of the population is below the poverty line.

"The residential concentration of poverty," contends Minnesota State Representative Myron Orfield, "creates social repercussions far greater than the sum of its parts. Physical separation from jobs and middle-class role models . . . reinforces social isolation and weakens work skills. Poor individuals who live in concentrated poverty are far more likely to become pregnant as teenagers, to drop out of high school, and to remain jobless than their counterparts in socioeconomically mixed neighborhoods."

Neighborhoods with strong community development organizations have not escaped the growth in concentrated poverty. As David Rusk has shown, average poverty rates increased from 23 percent to 25 percent in areas served by a sample group of "new" community development corporations (formed in the 1970s) and from 19 percent to 28 percent in areas served by a sample group of "old" CDCs (formed in the 1960s). Neighborhoods grew poorer not because low-income families moved in, but because so many middle-class households moved out.

The Changing Nature of Metropolitan Economies

In many respects the flip side of the rise in concentrated urban poverty is the surge in suburban and exurban sprawl. Metropolitan areas country-wide are seeing similar patterns of development—explosive sprawl where farmland and open space once reigned, matched by decline and abandonment in the central cities and older suburbs.

Between 1970 and 1990, for example, the population of the Chicago metropolitan area increased only 4 percent, but the land in the region used for urban purposes grew 35 percent. More than 450 square miles, twice the size of the city of Chicago, were converted from agricultural to urban use.

Even metropolitan areas that lost people gained land. The population of greater Pittsburgh fell 9 percent during 1970–90, but the land used for urban purposes grew 30 percent. Some 180 square miles of prime farmland in western Pennsylvania switched to urban use.

The exponential growth of suburban and exurban areas has two huge implications for community organizations working in urban neighborhoods. First, the suburbs are the principal job generators in the new economy. "In the early 1990s," according to the "State of the Cities" report, "87 percent of the new jobs in the lower paying and lower skilled service and retail trade sectors were created in the suburbs." Not surprisingly, jobless rates in central cities are generally one-third to one-half higher than those in nearby suburbs. Second, cities continue to lose middle-class families. Though only eleven of the thirty largest cities in 1970 have grown in the intervening years, all have seen heavy growth in the share of their population with low incomes.

Federal, state, and local government policies have all contributed to the growing spatial isolation of minority poverty that poses such a challenge to community-based institutions.

Government housing policies are a prime example. Until recently, the rules governing admission to public and assisted housing allowed the poorest households to jump to the top of the waiting lists. The result should have been predictable: the average income in public housing plummeted—from 33 percent of area median in 1980 to 17 percent ($6,500 for the average family) in 1994. Other rules made it hard for public housing agencies to tear down obsolete projects, even when it cost less to replace than to rehabilitate them. In many central cities, public housing became the locus of concentrated poverty in unsafe, indecent, and unsanitary conditions—the very opposite of what was intended.

Even the federal voucher program has fallen short of its goal of giving low-income families maximum choice in the private rental market. Most public housing agencies (which have a monopoly over voucher administration) treat vouchers as a "stepchild" program, rarely performing the landlord outreach or recipient counseling that spells success. In many metropolitan areas, as many as ten to fifteen public housing agencies pose bureaucratic obstacles to residents wishing to escape high-poverty areas. Suburban jurisdictions have erected their own barriers to mobility by favoring very low density settlements with little affordable rental housing. And racial hostility and discrimination, overt and covert, continue apace, as HUD found with suburban and congressional reaction to its Moving to Opportunity initiative. As the Urban Institute's Marge Turner has shown, despite housing vouchers' mobility potential, in some jurisdictions recipients are heavily concentrated in areas of high poverty.

Federal and state policies also continue to encourage exurban expansion—and with it the exodus of jobs and middle class families from central cities and older suburbs. Among such policies are federal and state spending on transportation, water, sewer, and other infrastructure; federal tax subsidies for homeownership; state land use laws; state incentives to major employers to relocate and expand to "greenfields" far outside central cities and older suburbs; federal rules that prohibit or impede reinvestment in central city neighborhoods with high minority concentrations; federal decisions on the location of government facilities and the procurement of government services; and federal laws and regulations regarding the environment, telecommunications, and utilities.

In short, despite often remarkable achievements, it is clear that community institutions will never realize their full potential unless and until the federal and state governments revamp policies that undermine community action.

Restructure Federal Housing Policies

Washington has already begun to overhaul problematic housing policies. In fact, the Clinton administration has embarked on the most ambitious reform of public housing since the program's inception in the 1930s. In an effort that will change the physical face of public housing, the administration plans to demolish some 100,000 public housing units—about one-twelfth of the entire public housing stock—by the year 2000. Creative replacement efforts are under way in dozens of cities, with heavy emphasis on smaller-scale, economically integrated affordable housing developments.

The reforms will also alter the human face of public housing. At the administration's behest, Congress has temporarily repealed the rules favoring the poorest households. Public housing agencies are being encouraged to create "mixed income" developments through admission policies that include working families as well as efforts to help existing residents increase their own incomes.

The same reformist impulses are needed in the housing voucher program if it is to succeed in giving low-income residents the choice to live where they want. Governance of the program—which now resides in 3,400 bureaucracies operating in parochial jurisdictions—must be shifted to the metropolitan level, as has been done, at least partially, for transportation and the environment. Such a shift would generate savings for the cash-strapped federal government by ending the wasteful duplication of administrative overhead. But even more important, it would move more lower-income residents into housing of their choice by requiring metropolitan administrators to provide counseling to potential recipients, outreach aggressively to capable landlords, and work with suburban churches and other groups to help place willing residents. Public housing agencies (or consortia of such agencies) should be allowed to compete for administrative responsibilities along with regional nonprofit organizations.

Federal Reform Infrastructure Policy

In regions across the country, the costs of unfettered sprawl are bringing together diverse coalitions of central city and older suburban elected officials, downtown business leaders, environmentalists, farmland preservation advocates, and civic, religious, and community groups. These coalitions are forcing state and metropolitan consideration of an eclectic mix of solutions—labor mobility, residential mobility, regional tax equity and stability, land use reform, and targeted investment of government subsidies.

Minnesota, for example, has upgraded metropolitan governance in the Twin Cities area and has enacted laws to spread the cost of poverty through the Twin Cities region. Maryland has recently enacted Governor Glendening's "smart growth" legislative package, which steers billions of state road, sewer, and school monies away from farms and open spaces to existing areas targeted for concentrated growth. Colorado, Delaware, and other states are now considering versions of smart growth to curb sprawl in their own backyards.

Washington should be a partner, not just an observer, in these efforts. It should enhance moves toward state and metropolitan solutions that curb sprawl, promote smart growth, rebuild established communities, and redress inequities between rich and poor political jurisdictions. This year, for example, Congress should do three simple things to improve federal transportation law—the most strategic point for intervention.

First, Congress should preserve and strengthen, not scale back, the existing metropolitan role in transportation planning and spending. Metropolitan areas are where transportation, land use, economic development, and environmental issues come together in practical ways.

Second, Congress should strengthen the role of citizens and communities in transportation decisions. It should require state and metropolitan transportation entities to disclose their spending patterns by political jurisdiction, use computer mapping tools to illustrate the disparate patterns, and make such information widely available. Such "right to know" laws already govern housing, banking, and the environment.

Finally, Congress should reward states and regions that make smart growth a central part of their transportation mission. It could provide regulatory relief or supplemental funding, or it could make direct grants to state and metropolitan entities to integrate transportation and land use planning.

Regional Strategies for CDCs

Change cannot be limited, however, to government policies. Community-based groups themselves must expand their horizons and build on their affordable housing successes.

First, community institutions need to place their neighborhood strategies in a regional context, understanding how government policies interact with the larger economy and engaging, where appropriate, on metropolitan issues and decisionmaking. As California scholars Manuel Pastor, Peter Dreier, and Gene Grigsby have recently noted, "Most community development groups have tended to favor a neighborhood focus because it fits their size, administrative capacity, and political base. The new challenges of persistent poverty, economic restructuring, and demographic transition," they note, "now require that communities reach out to a regional level of decisionmaking—and CDCs are probably the best placed vehicle in terms of expertise and credibility to lead this shift in policy paradigms."

Community institutions also need to help connect residents of their distressed neighborhoods to jobs in the metropolitan area. As Jeremy Nowak of the Delaware Valley Community Investment Fund has written, community groups must "shift their view of the neighborhoods they work in, seeing them primarily not as real estate and social service markets, but as labor markets." They need to learn "where people work, what their skills are, what the barriers to employment are, and which training programs or schools best link them to employers."

Some community development organizations are already expanding their focus to include work force development and access to employment. Indianapolis, for example, is contracting with community development corporations to help move welfare recipients to jobs. The federal government can help replicate these successful efforts through reforms in employment training laws as well as additional resources for community-based welfare-to-work efforts. Community groups can also expand their ties with corporate benefactors to include work force connections.

Community institutions are an essential building block of national urban and metropolitan policy. Yet their work is being consistently undermined by a series of government policies that push jobs and middle class people out of central cities, leaving only the very poor behind.

Government efforts must do more, therefore, than directly support the activities of community institutions; that is community policy on the cheap. Government must help create the urban economic climate in which community-based efforts can succeed.

Although the brief checklist of reforms I have noted in government housing and infrastructure would help ease the concentration of urban poverty, spur reinvestment in older established communities, and connect low-income urban residents to jobs in the metropolitan economy, that checklist is hardly complete. As Michael Porter, of the Harvard Business School, has persuasively argued, low-income urban neighborhoods have their own competitive market advantages that must be understood and exploited. Educational reform, land use reform, public safety efforts, and home ownership initiatives also demand serious attention and action. Nevertheless, the checklist presents a useful and necessary starting point for a community policy that can match the heady rhetoric of our national debates with the harsh reality of our urban streets.

10

Recreating the Civil Society One Child at a Time

COLIN L. POWELL

IT WAS A HAPPY coincidence that the Presidents' Summit for America's Future, which was held in Philadelphia this past April, should have been convened at a time when so many Americans are asking how we can reinvigorate our sense of civic virtue. Conceptions of what constitutes a "civil society" may differ as to details, but most people would probably agree that, at a minimum, a civil society is one whose members care about each other and about the well-being of the community as a whole.

What the Presidents' Summit did was to crystallize this concern around a coherent program aimed at helping our nation's youth. During my travels throughout the country, visiting inner-city neighborhoods and talking to the kids I've met there, I have been struck again and again by the stark differences between their childhoods and my own. When I was growing up in the Bronx, I wasn't rich—at least not in a material sense—but I had the matchless blessing of being reared by two devoted parents, backed up by a platoon of doting aunts and uncles, who gave me the love, discipline, and motivation I needed to succeed.

Too many of today's kids are not getting the same kind of nurturing environment that I—and most Americans—once took for granted. Too many of today's kids are growing up in dysfunctional families. Too many are being lost to child abuse, street violence, and other social pathologies. Too many are having children while they are still children themselves. Too many are dropping out of school or are not getting the quality of education they need to get good jobs when they graduate. As a result, too many kids are growing up unable to find their places in today's complex, information-driven economy. Too many are heading for stunted lives of dependency or crime.

As many as 15 million youngsters are "at risk" in today's America. They are in danger of being lost for good unless the more fortunate among us step forward and lend a hand. At the Presidents' Summit in Philadelphia, hundreds of our nation's leaders endorsed five basic resources that our young people need to become successful adults: an ongoing relationship with a caring adult or mentor; safe places to learn and grow during nonschool hours; a healthy start and a healthy future; a marketable skill through effective education; and an opportunity to give back through community service. The Summit participants pledged to make these resources available to at least 2 million youths by the year 2000. An ongoing campaign called America's Promise, which I chair, has been launched to redeem that pledge.

The response to our appeal has been highly gratifying. Nonprofit organizations, service clubs, educational institutions, houses of faith, corporations, and businesses large and small have all come forward to help us put the five resources in reach of needy youngsters.

McDonalds–Ronald McDonald House Charities have committed $100 million to an ambitious program supporting all five basic resources. The Oracle Corporation has also made a $100 million commitment to endow Oracle's Promise—a new foundation devoted to putting a computer on every child's desk in grades K–12 in the United States. Allstate is increasing its support for the Boys and Girls Clubs of America and the company's own "Street Smart" program. Other companies are giving employees paid time off to do volunteer work in their communities. Timberland, for example, is giving its employees forty hours of compensated leave a year. NationsBank is establishing twenty-five "Make a Difference Centers" to provide after-school programs for thousands of youngsters, including one-on-one homework assistance and tutoring.

The list of givers is growing longer all the time. Moreover, 30 states and nearly 180 communities have announced their own summits in support of this effort. Some state and local summits have already been held. Through these grass-roots efforts, we are helping the next generation of Americans to grow up to be good citizens, and we are reacquainting the present generation of Americans with the need to break down the barriers of race, class, and politics that divide us—which will help make us a more united and caring nation.

America's Promise cannot restore the civil society by itself. But rallying Americans around a campaign to help young people get a decent start in life is a big step in the right direction.

11

No Paintbrushes, No Paint

JANE R. EISNER

LAST JANUARY, when the presidential summit on community service was still on the drawing board, there was a renewed attempt to turn the national holiday for Martin Luther King Jr. into a real day of service. A day on, not a day off, its supporters said. I took it seriously—not only as a journalist, but as a mother of three school-age girls. Which is why, early on the morning of January 20, I filled up the van with my kids and their friends and drove to a dilapidated church in North Philadelphia to . . . serve.

We arrived at the appointed hour and were told to sit in the cavernous, second-floor space that needed a good scrub—and more—before it could be transformed into a meeting room for a drug and alcohol rehab center. There we waited and waited. The room filled with a rainbow of chattering students and adults, white and black, city and suburban, Catholic, Jewish, and Muslim. All waiting.

Finally, an hour and a half later, we were given a rousing sermon and put to work. Only there weren't enough paintbrushes, or ladders, or rollers to paint the alcove. There weren't enough new squares of carpet to replace the old ones. Nor enough frames for the posters. The older kids managed to keep occupied; my seven-year-old felt useless. We left mid-day, half satisfied that we made, perhaps, a small contribution.

That evening, I asked my youngest daughter as I put her to bed: "Wouldn't it be great if next year all the kids in your grade volunteered on King Day?"

"But, Mom," she replied, "will there be something to do?"

Her question has haunted me ever since, as I have seen the nation fall in love with the promise and potential of addressing the needs of its young through community service. I, too, am enchanted by the goodness it evokes, the opportunity to help the less fortunate, to overcome the isolation that grips too many of us, comfortable in our neighborhoods, ready to hide behind busy lives. I've done enough volunteer work to know that it doesn't always produce tangible results; sometimes, it's the doing that makes a difference.

But now that the hype and hoopla of the Presidents' Summit has come and gone, I am still worried that good intentions and unrealistic expectations are going to beat out common sense. And common sense dictates that unless community service is employed wisely, it won't make any more of a difference than we did at the North Philadelphia church. Sometimes, it can even do more harm than good.

Volunteer work, if done right, is work, with complexity and consequence. If not done right, it can accomplish nothing or, worse, it can leave the lonely and suffering even more bereft, and blunt the passion in those wishing to serve.

Good Intentions Are Not Enough

More than good intentions are necessary if community service is going to help feed, heal, teach, and mentor those in need. There must be an infrastructure. Now, the eloquent preacher who runs the drug rehab center should not be blamed for the paucity of paintbrushes or carpet squares. It's his job to turn around lives, not organize cleanups. But somebody—from a local business, perhaps?—should have scoured the scene a week earlier, sized up the need, purchased all the necessary supplies, and prepared for the influx of volunteers.

Thomas McKenna, national executive director of Big Brothers/Big Sisters of America, has faced this issue: his widely recognized mentoring program was sometimes chided for being carefully slow and small. "There's a mystical notion people have that if you throw volunteers at kids, something's going to happen," he said earlier this year in Philadelphia, where the national headquarters is based. "Not true. You need the infrastructure. People don't understand or value what it takes to orient and train volunteers and to support the mentoring relationship after the match. It's not glitzy, but you need it."

It's not just kids who need it. The elderly do as well. Judith Rodin, president of the University of Pennsylvania, has written about research done by a colleague in a Pittsburgh nursing home in the 1970s. Some of the elderly residents were visited occasionally by local undergraduates, according to no schedule. Other residents were allowed to set the time and duration of the visits.

Perhaps not surprisingly, the elderly who had been put in control were more alert and in better health. When the study was over, students went home for spring break and the visits ended. A year and a half later, the researchers returned to the nursing home and made a startling finding: more of the residents with control had died than had the others.

When the contact and attention that the elderly themselves had controlled abruptly stopped—even though they were warned that it would—the effects were profound. They were left with less than nothing.

Does this mean that students should immediately stop visiting elderly residents of nursing homes? Of course not. But the visits must be shaped into the context of the lives of the elderly. Don't give without preparing for what happens when you take away—especially from a vulnerable, needy population.

The main goal of volunteer work isn't to make the volunteer feel better, although that is a hoped-for consequence. It's to accomplish something that other private or public sources cannot and to enhance the volunteer's sense of responsibility to the greater community. Benjamin Barber, director of the Walt Whitman Center for the Culture and Politics of Democracy at Rutgers University, says the approach a volunteer brings to the work is most important.

Is she there out of a sense of noblesse oblige, to do something charitable without addressing the underlying problem? Barber tells of a student who, after a year volunteering in a homeless shelter, said, "This was the most extraordinary experience I've ever had. I just hope my children will have a chance to do it." (And I guess we all should hope the homeless will still be around to give our kids the same warm glow.)

Or is she there in a spirit of partnership, to serve an immediate need and to work toward a time when her children won't have to help out at a shelter because most homelessness will have been prevented? The volunteer's long-term goal should not be to perpetuate her role but to make it superfluous.

Barber tells another story that drives home the need to place community service in context. His Rutgers students were divided into groups to work on specific service projects. Some were sent to work at a homeless shelter, others to paint the plugs of fire hydrants in a nearby community.

After a couple of weeks, the painting crew complained. This is community service? We should be helping the needy, not painting hydrants! Barber then had the students meet with an official from the community, and his explanation made all the difference.

It turns out that the community's firefighters had wanted the plugs painted because it would help them locate the plugs more quickly when the hydrants were knee-high in snow and ice. It was a particularly urgent job because the previous year, a year of heavy winter weather, two residents may have died in fires because the hydrant plugs were so difficult to find. And the community itself didn't have the money to pay municipal workers do the job.

Once given the context, the students returned to the work with zeal, convinced that they were contributing to a healthier community.

So volunteer work must be placed in its proper context. It must be well coordinated and targeted to help a specific need. And, finally, it must be recognized for what it is: often an enormous help but not often a replacement for the public or private sector responsibility. It certainly has its limitations.

The Germantown Avenue Cleanup

Consider the situation on Philadelphia's Germantown Avenue as an illustration of that last point. The long, important thoroughfare that winds through some of Philadelphia's seediest neighborhoods was the scene of a massive volunteer cleanup on the day before the Presidents' Summit. The *Inquirer's* Marc Kaufman returned to the street a week later, and here's what he found.

Although more than 6,000 people registered to work that day, and hundreds were turned away because there were no more work slots left, neon-colored tags—"work orders" instructing volunteers to clean or paint over graffiti—still covered blocks of storefronts and restaurants and scores of rowhouse walls. City officials acknowledged that 20 to 25 percent of the work orders were not finished. And a fair number of the walls that were cleaned had to be revisited by paid city crews, because of the poor work quality. One storefront, for instance, was a motley patchwork of light blue, dark blue, gray, and yellow.

There were several reasons for the spotty performance. Trucks couldn't always get through Secret Service barricades to distribute paint and rollers. Relatively few local residents joined outside volunteers in the southern, hardest-hit stretch of Germantown Avenue. And hard-to-reach graffiti were deliberately left for city crews to deal with.

But the underlying reason, Kaufman reported, is that much volunteer work is inherently inefficient. Most volunteers aren't as skilled, as focused, or as productive as paid professionals—especially at a massive effort like this, one that attracted the president and so many other distracting celebrities. Donna Cooper, who organized the Germantown Avenue cleanup and is now a deputy mayor, said, "I think the conclusion is unavoidable—volunteer work is great, but it is very inefficient and can seldom do the job as well as a paid staff. That's no rap on volunteers, who did a terrific job. That's just reality."

And remember: as volunteer efforts go, cleaning up Germantown Avenue or the church in North Philadelphia is relatively easy and requires far less commitment than mentoring or tutoring a child. Painting a building doesn't demand the same dedication and skill as the delicate, difficult job of helping to turn around a young life. That's not an activity for a Sunday morning in the sun.

If the growing gap between government action and public need is going to be filled through community service, then the limitations and realities of volunteer work must be recognized. This is not said to dull any of the spirit of the summit or diminish the extraordinary work done by volunteers nationwide, whose sense of citizenship compelled them to help the needy long before the bunting went up on Independence Hall. My hope is that serving others should become a natural part of life for every American, as long as it does more good than harm.

12

Beyond Theory
Civil Society in Action

PAM SOLO AND GAIL PRESSBERG

MORE THAN two hundred years ago, English philosopher John Locke wrote in *The Second Treatise of Civil Government,* "The only way by which any one divests himself of his natural liberty and puts on the bonds of civil society is by agreeing with other men to join and unite into a community."

In America, particularly during the late twentieth century, we have been negotiating those bonds on a scale that Locke probably could not have imagined. We continue to combine these mutually exclusive elements—freedom and obligation—in ever new and unprecedented ways. In the past three decades we have increasingly placed emphasis on the former rather than the latter, systematically altering the way we think about women's roles, racial divisions, sexual mores, and class stratification. In so doing, we have added and interpreted laws in accordance with our growing bias in favor of individual rights and tried to create social policy to preserve those rights. In redefining to what and to whom we owe our allegiances in light of these notions about personal freedom, we have gradually changed the rules governing all of our fundamental relationships, community and family ties being no exception.

As people started considering their personal and professional options in a way never before possible, there was no denying that an epidemic of estrangement overtook America. Some called it liberation while others considered it deterioration. Conservatives, observing this sea-change, warned of imminent social disaster and talked about recapturing the best of the past. They embraced traditional values and argued vehemently for the restoration of clearly understood public morality. They blamed liberals—the alleged architects of this radical transformation—for what they viewed as America's decay. Conservatives, pointing to what they saw as the by-products of familial break-down—increased crime, drug use, and teen pregnancy, among other societal ills—campaigned for programs and policies that they believed would reinforce the integrity of the family unit. They encouraged people to resist the siren call of excessive individualism, ridiculing their more "permissive" opponents for their destructive self-interestedness and overbearing secularism.

Liberals, however, cited these greater personal freedoms as boons for society. Never before had so many different groups had access, albeit limited access, to America's power structures. Society was just experiencing growing pains, and if things were bad it was because we hadn't come far enough in eliminating the obstacles that continued to prevent these historically disadvantaged groups from gaining a solid foothold in the middle class. Liberals, citing the very same social ills the Conservatives had—crime, drug use, and illegitimacy—blamed their political counterparts for dismissing the economic component inherent in all these troubles. Poverty, not permissiveness, was the source of society's most intractable problems, they claimed. They believed that it was the job of government to act as intermediary for the people straining toward still greater freedom and equality.

Although there has always been a struggle for our nation's ideological helm among an assortment of captains all of whom claim to know the best direction in which to steer our country, of late—perhaps in the last decade—we have been led to believe that contemporary America has become a nation in the midst of a culture war. If the media accounts are to be believed, the years have taken their toll; apathy and acrimony have eaten away at our sense of community and left us in a sorry state. We remain wed to our narrow interests and lull ourselves into complacency with the help of our television sets.

We take issue with this portrayal. Our work at the Institute for Civil Society (ICS) has allowed us a privileged view of civil society in action, and we have found that in most communities across the United States, the political philosophies of both liberals and conservatives simply miss the rich, nuanced, and complex ways in which average Americans balance the needs of communities with the needs of individuals. As Alan Wolfe demonstrates in *One Nation, After All*, the ostensible divisiveness in public life has occurred largely at rarified levels, among the elite members of the press corps and between opposing political camps. The ideological jousting that so preoccupies pundits and politicians seems to be of little concern to most ordinary Americans. A vibrant and lively civil society flourishes in spite of the contentious, often rancorous, public discourse. Perhaps people have turned from bowling together to problem solving together, the emphasis, of course, being on togetherness.

This navigation between self-interest and the interests of others is never perfect and never finished. That is what civil society means: it is the place where people, neighborhoods, and communities define, mediate, and argue as they work to forge consensus. The common theme in all these struggles is empowerment, both for the individual and the community as a whole. How exactly are communities working together?

—The Family Support Network, founded by Cheryl Honey, a former welfare mother, began as a small database in Bothell, Washington, which listed people and organizations able to support families in times of crisis. It is now a fully developed "yellow pages" that links community members and more than 800 people in the Seattle area who share resources and do volunteer work. FSN also has its own FM radio program, "I Can Do That," which not only matches service providers with those in need of services, but also focuses on policy issues. Communities across the United States are inviting Honey and her colleagues to help them set up their own FSNs.

—The pollution that spoils our rivers cannot be reversed merely by government action alone. The River Watch Network brings river communities together to learn about and protect their rivers. Working with RWN, community groups such as schools, businesses, service clubs, state and local government agencies, and conservation groups analyze ecosystems and create strategies to conserve rivers. A Rio Grande/Rio Bravo pilot project in Texas uses thirty trained volunteers, ten of whom are now Texas-certified water quality monitors to sample water twice monthly at nine sites, focusing on the health effects of using contaminated waters. Next year RWN plans to target other affected rivers and the communities surrounding them.

—Will the drug pusher or the minister be the first adult a teenager meets as they leave the corridors of their high school at day's end? The Ten Point Coalition is a national organization of African-American ministers targeting at-risk youth in their own communities. The coalition, modeled on Boston's Ten Point Coalition, reaches out to the most troubled young people, "adopting" gangs, patrolling neighborhoods, counseling victims, and using churches as community centers. By forming partnerships with social service agencies and law enforcement officers, the coalition has significantly reduced violence by local youths. The Ten Point Coalition in Dorchester, Massachusetts, is also working to create new entrepreneurial businesses run by former gang members who in turn employ other former gang members.

—Who will initiate the revitalization of our urban areas? In nearby Brockton, Massachusetts, 5,000 families from sixteen synagogues and churches formed the Brockton Interfaith Community (BIC) in 1989 to tackle major issues including crime, neighborhood revitalization, employment training, transportation, and youth concerns. Funded by the Campaign for Human Development of the U.S. Catholic Conference, BIC succeeded in stabilizing neighborhoods by encouraging homeownership. Using its strength as a neighborhood-based coalition, BIC negotiated a package with area banks to lower interest rates, worked to eliminate the need for private mortgage insurance (PMI), and convinced the city to provide a municipal subsidy for the first ten years of a mortgage. The mayor of Brockton, in his 1997 State of the City address, cited BIC as one of the groups responsible for revitalizing the city.

—Men who have served long sentences in New York state prisons run the Harlem Justice Center, a secular counterpart of the Ten Point Coalition. These men reach out to would-be predators through recreational activities, individual and group counseling, and frank talk about life in prison. Their central message is that taking personal responsibility for one's actions is the first step in any successful rehabilitation process.

—Stop Handgun Violence, a coalition composed of the family members of victims who died as a result of handgun violence, has a long list of major accomplishments since its inception in 1995. Their 252-foot billboard on the Massachusetts Turnpike near Boston's Fenway Park displays pictures of children who were killed by handguns and cannot help but have a major impact on its 250,000 daily viewers. As a result of this organization's educational activities, Massachusetts will be the first state to ban "Saturday Night Specials," the type of gun involved in more than 50 percent of all gun deaths. Recognizing that an outright ban on handguns may be impossible to achieve, other groups working to prevent handgun violence have proposed legislation requiring that guns kept in the home be secured and inaccessible to children; provide gun owners with free trigger locks in order to render them inoperable by children and burglars; and promote the development of "smart" guns that are rendered inoperable if fired by anyone other than their owners.

—Can small businesses be developed to create new, meaningful, and decently paid jobs? Can the nonprofit sector play a role in providing the training and capital necessary to support the creation of small businesses? To Market, To Market, a new project of the Women's Educational and Industrial Union (WEIU), a group founded 120 years ago, identifies underrepresented and low-income women with products to sell and facilitates their access to the market. The WEIU's Shop supports the efforts of these vendors to develop and market their products in a variety of ways: by representing their products in the shop, by referring them to other potential markets, and by providing guidance and direction in product development, packaging, distribution, marketing, and promotion. Critical to the success of To Market, To Market is the development of a collaborative relationship with local community-based organizations. For example, the Dorchester Bay Economic Development Corporation (serving one of the more financially strapped communities in the Boston area) and the South End Community Health Center's Trabajo de Mujeres make referrals to To Market, To Market.

—While most not-for-profit institutions provide social and educational services that are critical to our nation's health and well-being, in an age of increasing disenfranchisement and poverty, how do we create mediating institutions that work for a democratic redistribution of power? Recreating Congregations for the 21st Century, a project of the Industrial Areas Foundation, is working with 300 congregations representing 14 denominations in California, Oregon, and the state of Washington to build effective "mediating institutions." The goal of the program is to build social capital to give people a greater sense of belonging and participation. They provide an instrument for engaging in sustained public life. Intermediary institutions, at their best, are instigators, creators, and protectors. They defend the interests of their members and surrounding communities, helping to create social, economic, spiritual, political, and economic capital to benefit their community.

One of the flagship organizations, United Neighborhoods Organization (UNO), provides an opportunity for its members to "live" their faith. From creating nonpartisan candidate forums for the recent Los Angeles city council election, to negotiating with the Immigration and Naturalization Service (INS) to cut the time it takes to process citizenship applications by at least six months; to mobilizing parishioners to block a toxic waste treatment plant slated to open near a Huntington Park high school; to clearing prostitutes from neighborhood streets, the UNO is an organization of Los Angeles neighborhood parishes. The main benefit of membership in UNO for parishes is the guarantee of help with local problems and training in how to hold politicians and business leaders accountable for their actions.

The participants in these community initiatives share the conviction that problem solving cannot be left to others. Effective government programs can make things better. But the best government policies have emerged from collaborative efforts among government, community institutions, and the private sector. Enduring social changes are not simply legislated by government. They arise from social action rooted in individual responsibility and accountability.

In 1928 presidential candidate Herbert Hoover rallied delegates to the Republican party convention at Madison Square Garden in support of an American system of rugged individualism. Thirty-two years later, John F. Kennedy summoned a different image of the American system standing "on the edge of a new frontier" and challenging Americans to ask what they could do for their country, not what their country could do for them. As Hoover saw it, rugged individualism is what America *is*, not simply a characteristic of immigrants seeking a new nation of freedom from monarchies or political repression. Kennedy aimed to steer the nation beyond the individual to a new era of common cause.

Since then, grass-roots groups have been making their way through turbulent times, drawing on their resources as individuals to create and recreate their communities year after year. In this century we have learned that total systems of control cannot permanently repress or stifle the individual spirit. We are also learning that community and a sense of belonging to a local place have no substitute in the global economy. Human beings—even the most rugged individualists—require a web of relations; they need to be supported by organizations and institutions in order to thrive. In speaking of our civil "bonds" perhaps Locke was acknowledging the paradox familiar to every person who has ever found personal fulfillment through reaching out to others: it is when we give that we receive.

13

Poverty 101

What Liberals and Conservatives Can Learn from Each Other

DAVID KUO

THE TWENTY-FIRST century has already begun with a radical new welfare system that fundamentally changes how America cares for her poor, dependent, jobless, and abused. The 1996 welfare reform law was the result of a decade of often dramatic and contentious debate about the proper nature of reform. On the one side were conservative reformers who demanded work requirements, illegitimacy prevention, and general de-entitlement. On the other were liberal reformers who also had an interest in work requirements and better job placement but wanted to see the essential characteristics of the social safety net remain intact.

The heat of the last debate was often painfully intense, but perhaps the lull before the next welfare debate begins will afford both camps of reformers the opportunity to learn from each other—especially when it comes to the hard work of recreating civil society and a private sector approach to caring for those individuals in need.

Liberals first. Faith matters. Ironically for a liberal welfare tradition that had its roots in religious revival, many of today's liberals acknowledge that religious faith is certainly a matter of importance, while ignoring—or being actively hostile to—its policy potential as a catalyst for radical change in people's lives.

During the last welfare debate, for instance, Senator John Ashcroft's "charitable choice" provision to allow states to contract with private and religious charitable organizations using federal funds was broadly attacked by many on the left. Yet its basic purpose was simply to level the playing field for faith-based not-for-profits.

Overwhelming evidence coming from groups as diverse as the Heritage Foundation and Public/Private Ventures suggests that faith is not only important, it may be the factor in determining whether an at-risk child, a welfare mother, or a convicted criminal is able to turn his or her life around. It is vital that political liberals embrace this idea. The next year will give them opportunities to do so: new efforts to encourage this kind of religious element in welfare include the charity tax credit and further implementation of charitable choice–type measures.

Conservatives next. Governmental programs can do—and have done—good. In just the past few decades, hunger and malnutrition have become far less serious social problems thanks to food stamps. Where once one out of every three elderly Americans was in poverty, today that number has dropped to about one in ten, thanks to the indexing of social security benefits and medicare. These are social policy successes virtually without parallel.

Despite its well-documented failures, the War on Poverty changed the face of poverty. The lesson for conservatives is that keeping intact a safety net of noncash services for the poor—and especially for the children—is crucial to preventing future welfare dependency. In a recent book, *What Money Can't Buy*, University of Chicago professor Susan Mayer pointed out that the two most important things determining a child's future are, first, that his or her basic needs be met, and, second, that he or she be the child of parents with character. Legislatively, little can be done to ensure the second. Realistically, improving the delivery mechanisms for programs like medicaid so that those who use the services will have better care and better access should be at the forefront of the conservative agenda.

Liberals need to place more trust in the private sector. Long skeptical of some conservative claims that the private sector could replace decades-old government programs overnight, some liberals appear to believe that the private sector can actually do very little—while clinging to the belief that true compassion is directly related to federal spending on welfare. In fact, free market charity and social entrepreneurism operating without the debilitating effects of government are the real hopes for making a transformational difference.

Looking to examples like the "He Is Pleased" program in Delaware, founded by mutual fund magnate Foster Friess, the evidence is apparent that the social sector is a market like any other—with one difference: here the profit isn't financial, it is personal. He Is Pleased helps homeless men and women make the transition from the streets into full-time employment. Started with venture capital from Friess several years ago, HIP has already helped about one hundred homeless people change their lives. Grounded in hard work—a ninety-day cycle of paid work cleaning up the city—and tough rules—tardiness is not accepted, drug tests are mandatory—HIP is a social sector equivalent to microcorporations like Apple or Sun Microsystems twenty years ago. It is cutting-edge, it is optimistic, and it is providing a challenge to established forms of charity. Scores of programs like these have sprung up across the country—they are the best hope for change and need to be supported.

Conservatives must not trust blindly in the private sector. One temptation to which conservatives sometimes succumb is believing that all government programs are bad and all private charity programs are good. Both are quite untrue.

Conservatives ought not to paint too rosy a picture of private sector charity. Rhetorically, they asked Americans to choose between government and charity, HUD or Habitat for Humanity, HHS or the Red Cross, knowing the answer they would get. But in so doing, they ignored the reality that many of the biggest and best-known organizations—groups with multibillion dollar budgets and national recognition—have served as little more than private sector surrogates of the welfare state. Groups like the United Way, the Red Cross, and Catholic Charities receive a substantial portion of their funding from the federal government. Not coincidentally, they also tend to reflect in mission, means, and orientation the government model of impersonal, bureaucratic, and secular assistance that is a far cry from the kind of assistance people need. Conservatives who have been at the forefront of critiquing government should now be at the forefront of critiquing the private sector—of pointing out the good, the noble, and the bad. The recently completed National Commission on Philanthropy and Civic Renewal took a much-needed step in this direction.

Liberals need to better appreciate the importance of work—all work. Too often liberals have focused on the availability of "good" jobs to the exclusion of encouraging employment. Belittling "low-wage" jobs as demeaning, intentionally or unintentionally they sent a message that work, in and of itself, is not that important—that only "good" jobs count. Conservatives, for their part, need to consider the barriers to moving from welfare to work. Moving to a low-paying job can mean giving up medical benefits for one's children—a clear systemic barrier to work.

Most studies show that getting and keeping a job, any job, is the most essential step to beating poverty. Finding and keeping a job provides more than income. It provides a sense of self-worth and accomplishment. It does something else as well—it almost guarantees raises. Although liberals have focused on job training and job opportunities, they haven't focused enough on putting people to work—a sort of trial by employment fire. Early evidence from the states seems to suggest that for many people on welfare, the new welfare law provided the impetus to change. This is not to say that all have found work or will be able to, but it is an important lesson—one that, as Governor Thompson of Wisconsin has shown, sometimes requires state spending.

Poverty: A Grinding Reality

A final thought for conservatives. Poverty in America is real. Some on the right seem to suggest that poverty is just an invention of the left, that it is mostly a matter of sloth and bad bookkeeping.

While poverty may not be as life-threatening as it once was, it can still be dark and desperate. As accounts like *There Are No Children Here* and *Turning Stones* have shown, poverty is not just "poverty," though its ravages can turn children into "children"—kids who may be chronologically young but who have seen and experienced life that is beyond the nightmares of many adults.

Coming to grips with the reality of poverty in America may be the most important thing that conservatives can learn from liberals. Certainly it would change the tone of conservatism. Conservatives will have more success undoing the welfare state if they abandon arguments asserting that all of America's poor are either "undeserving" or "nonexistent."

The hope that liberals and conservatives can take the time to learn from each other on matters of poverty springs from the common ground they have already found in the need to strengthen America's civil sector. In just the past half decade, politicians, pundits, and professors from across the ideological spectrum have come to the recognition that the real hope of reform and the true answers to long-vexing social problems will come from "civil society."

That agreement is rooted in a common appreciation that communities and civic groups and churches have strengths and abilities beyond the dreams of government. They are actively and intimately involved in needy individuals' lives. They share a common code of moral responsibility that provides guidance and guardrails. They have elements of faith that touch people in a far more profound way than a check or a voucher.

If this kind of agreement could find a way to grow in the poisonous atmosphere of the last welfare debate, let us all hope that in this calm after the storm the two sides will come together even more closely and revivify our common lives.

14

Where Have All the Followers Gone?

ALAN EHRENHALT

There is a longing, among millions of Americans now reaching middle age, for a stable and secure social world that they believe existed during their childhoods and does not exist now. "I want to live in a place again where I can walk down any street without being afraid," Hillary Rodham Clinton said shortly after becoming First Lady. "I want to be able to take my daughter to a park at any time of day or night in the summer and remember what I used to be able to do when I was a little kid." Those sorts of feelings, and a nostalgia for the benefits of old-fashioned community life at the neighborhood level, form a sort of backdrop to middle class life at the end of this decade and century.

The very word community has found a place, however fuzzy and imprecise, all over the ideological spectrum. On the far left it is a code word for a more egalitarian society in which the oppressed of all colors are included and made the beneficiaries of a more generous social welfare system that commits far more than the current one does to education, social services, and the eradication of poverty. On the far right it signifies an emphasis on individual self-discipline that would replace the welfare state with a private rebirth of personal responsibility. In the middle it seems to reflect a much simpler yearning for a network of comfortable, reliable relationships.

But it has been all over the pages of popular journalism and political discourse in the 1990s.

Authority is something else again. It evokes no similar feelings of nostalgia. On the one hand, few would dispute that it has eroded over the last generation. Walk into a large public high school in a typical middle class suburb today, and you will see a principal who must spend huge portions of his or her day having to cajole recalcitrant students, teachers, and staff into accepting direction that, a generation ago, they would have accepted unquestioningly just because the principal was the principal and they were subordinates. You will see teachers who risk a profane response if they dare criticize one of their pupils.

Or consider the mainstream Protestant church. We haven't yet reached the point where parishioners curse their minister in the same way high-school students curse their teachers, but if it is even a faintly liberal congregation, there is a good chance that the minister has lost his title: he is no longer "Dr." but "Jim," or "Bob," or whatever his friends like to call him. Putting the minister on a level with his parishioners is one small step in the larger unraveling of authority.

Authority and community have in fact unraveled together. But authority possesses very few mourners. To most of the Americans in the baby boom generation, it will always be a word with sinister connotations, calling forth a rush of uncomfortable memories about the schools, churches, and families in which they grew up. Rebellion against those memories constituted the defining event of their generational lives. Wherever on the political spectrum this generation has landed, it has brought its suspicion of authority with it. "Authority," says P. J. O'Rourke, speaking for his baby boom cohort loud and clear, "has always attracted the lowest elements in the human race."

The suspicion of institutional authority and the enshrinement of individual choice are everywhere in the American society of the 1990s. They extend beyond the routines of our individual lives into the debates we conduct on topics as diverse as school reform and corporate management.

Of all the millions of words devoted in the past decade to the subject of educational change, few have suggested improving the schools by putting the rod back in the teacher's hand, or returning to a curriculum of required memorization and classroom drill. The center of the discussion is the concept of school choice: the right of families to decide for themselves which schools their children will attend. Many things may be said for and against the concept of school choice, but one point is clear enough—in education, as in virtually every other social enterprise, individual choice is the antithesis of authority. It is a replacement for it.

Similarly, one can comb the shelves of a bookstore crowded with volumes on corporate management without coming across one that defends the old-fashioned pyramid in which orders come down from the chief executive, military-style, and descend intact to the lower reaches of the organization. Some corporations still operate that way, but they are regarded as dinosaurs. Corporate hierarchies are out of fashion. The literature is all about constructing management out of webs rather than pyramids, about decentralizing the decision process, empowering people at all levels of the organization. The words "command and control" are the obscenities of present-day management writing.

As they are, more broadly, in economic thinking. Ten years ago, few Americans were familiar with the phrase "command economy." Now, virtually all of us know what it means. It is the definition of a society that fails because it attempts to make economic decisions by hierarchy rather than by the free choice of its individual citizens. It is the most broadly agreed-upon reason for the abject failure of world communism. The communist implosion both reinforced and seemed to validate our generational suspicions about hierarchy and authority in all their manifestations, foreign and domestic, the American CEOs and school principals of the 1950s almost as much as the dictators who made life miserable in authoritarian countries around the world.

What has happened in education and economics has also happened, not surprisingly, in the precincts of political thought. There has in fact been a discussion about authority among political philosophers in the past two decades, and its tone tells us something. It has been a debate in which scholars who profess to find at least some value in the concept have struggled to defend themselves against libertarian critics who question whether there is any such thing as legitimate authority at all, even for duly constituted democratic governments. "All authority is equally illegitimate," the philosopher Robert Paul Wolff wrote in a landmark 1971 book, *In Defense of Anarchy*. "The primary obligation of man," Wolff argued, "is autonomy, the refusal to be ruled." It is only a slight exaggeration to say that the record of debate on this subject in the twenty years since has consisted largely of responses to Wolff, most of them rather tentative and half-hearted.

If there were an intellectual movement of Authoritarians to match the Communitarians, they would be the modern equivalent of a subversive group. The elites of the country, left and right alike, would regard them as dangerous. The America of the 1990s may be a welter of confused values, but on one point we speak with unmistakable clarity: we have become emancipated from social authority as we used to know it.

We don't want the 1950s back. What we want is to edit them. We want to keep the safe streets, the friendly grocers, and the milk and cookies, while blotting out the political bosses, the tyrannical headmasters, the inflexible rules, and the lectures on 100 percent Americanism and the sinfulness of dissent. But there is no easy way to have an orderly world without somebody making the rules by which order is preserved. Every dream we have about recreating civil society in the absence of authority will turn out to be a pipe dream in the end.

This is a lesson that people who call themselves conservatives sometimes seem determined not to learn. There are many on the right who, while devoting themselves unquestioningly to the ideology of the free market, individual rights, and personal choice, manage to betray their longing for old-fashioned community and a world of lasting relationships. In the 1980s, Ronald Reagan was one of them. His 1984 re-election campaign, built around a series of "Morning Again in America" TV commercials featuring stage-set small-town Main Streets of the sort Reagan strolled down in youth and in Hollywood, was a small token of communitarian rhetoric in the midst of a decade of unraveling standards, economic and moral as well. But when people tell us markets and unlimited choice are good for communities and traditional values, the burden of proof is on them, not on us.

The disruptiveness of the market has taken away the neighborhood savings and loan, with its familiar veteran tellers, and set down in its place a branch of Citibank where no one has worked as long as a month and where even the oldest depositor has to slide his driver's license under the window. Market power has replaced the locally owned newspaper, in most of the cities in America, with a paper whose owner is a corporate executive far away and whose publisher is a middle manager stopping in town for a couple of years on his way to a higher position at headquarters.

Once McDonald's begins serving breakfast in a small community and siphoning off business from the Main Street cafe that always provided a morning social center, that cafe is very likely doomed. Once Wal-Mart turns up on the outskirts of town and undersells the local hardware and clothing stores, Main Street itself is in trouble. People do not want to destroy their historic town centers, but they are rarely willing to resist the siren call of cheaper light bulbs and underwear.

In its defense, one can say that the global market onslaught of the past two decades was technologically inevitable, or, more positively, that it is the best guarantor of individual freedom, and that individual freedom is the most important value for us to preserve. Or one can say that the market puts more dollars in the ordinary citizen's pocket, and that after all the bottom line should be the bottom line. But in the end there is no escaping the reality that the market is a force for disrupting existing relationships. To argue that markets are the true friend of community or civil society is an inversion of common sense. And to idealize markets and call oneself a conservative is to distort reality.

What is true of market worship is true in a larger sense of personal choice, the even more precious emblem of the baby boom generation. To worship choice and community together is to misunderstand what community is all about. Community means not subjecting every action in life to the burden of choice, but rather accepting the familiar and reaping the psychological benefits of having one fewer calculation to make in the course of the day.

Middle-aged people who are serious about promoting the communitarian values they associate with their childhoods, people like Hillary Clinton who insist they want their old neighborhoods back, need to rethink some of the most precious values they learned in the 1960s and have refused to discard. They need to consider that it is not always a good thing to be a creature of choice. Sometimes it is better to be a creature of habit—of prescription, to use the word that Russell Kirk liked to use."If we are to accomplish anything in this life," Kirk once wrote, "we must take much for granted."

Of course, there will be quite a few people to whom none of this makes any sense, people who believe that individual choice is the most important standard, period; that no society can ever get enough of it; that the problem in the last generation is not that we have abandoned authority but that there are still a few vestiges of it yet to be eradicated. Many of these people call themselves libertarians and arguing with them is complicated by the fact that they are nearly always intelligent, interesting, and personally decent. Libertarian ideas are seductive and would be nearly impossible to challenge if one thing were true—if we lived in a world full of P. J. O'Rourkes, all of us bright and articulate and individualistic and wanting nothing more than the freedom to try all the choices and experiments that life has to offer and express our individuality in an endless series of new and creative ways.

But this is the libertarian fallacy: the idea that the world is full of repressed libertarians, waiting to be freed from the bondage of rules and authority. Perhaps, if the libertarians were right, life would be more interesting. But what they failed to notice, as they squirmed awkwardly through childhood in what seemed to them the strait-jacket of school and family and church, is that most people are not like them. Most people want a chart to follow and are not happy when they don't have one, or when they learned one as children and later see people all around them ignoring it. Philosophers are free to debate the legitimacy of any set of rules as long as they wish, but it remains true, and in the end more important, that the uncharted life, the life of unrestricted choice and eroded authority, is one most ordinary people do not enjoy leading. In their view, the erosion of both community and authority in the last generation is not a matter of intellectual debate. It is something they can feel in their bones, and the feeling makes them shiver.

PART TWO
Political Responses

15

Civil Society and the Humble Role of Government

DAN COATS AND RICK SANTORUM

WHEN THE welfare reform bill was signed into law in the summer of 1996, both supporters and critics characterized it as one of the most important pieces of legislation in a generation. Regrettably, and precisely because of its importance, it was too often regarded as the conclusion of one critical policy debate, rather than the premise of another, equally critical discussion: what can the government effectively do, with some degree of public consensus, in the face of poverty and social disintegration?

What is required is an alternative vision of caring and compassion that recognizes the role private institutions can play in the wake of the welfare state's retrenchment. Those of us who supported welfare reform did not intend to abandon our most vulnerable citizens. We anticipated reducing a destructive dependency on government so that some of the most compelling social and spiritual needs of the poor could be met by those institutions originally equipped to do so: schools, neighborhoods, and churches. We now anticipate that those institutions can become more vital and play a larger role in our cultural rejuvenation.

In his book, *Democracy's Discontent*, Michael Sandel contrasts what he characterizes as a procedural democracy, which provides a neutral framework of individual rights within which citizens freely pursue their own ends, with the tradition of "republican political theory" that teaches that freedom is dependent on the ability of citizens to participate in self-rule. According to the republican tradition, government is not neutral toward the ends citizens pursue, and civic and moral ties precede liberty because they help to create a culture on which liberty depends and by which it is sustained. If we see the former Aid to Families with Dependent Children (AFDC) program as one of the expressions, even triumphs, of proceduralism—the state as guarantor of a minimum level of income (with which the recipient could pursue his or her own ends)—and little else, we could also see its overhaul as an opportunity to revivify those civic, community, and even religious ties that sustain a vital democracy because they help to create the habits of mind, character, and heart that render citizens capable of effective self-government.

For too long in modern America, politics and public debate has tended to focus on the role of government and on the rights of individuals. It has neglected the layer of institutions that raise our children, enforce an informal order in our neighborhoods, and even reclaim our lives when we fall and fail. It has long neglected the civilizing role of families and communities, charities and churches. Now, however, that neglect is ending, and both a grass-roots and intellectual revolution are reshaping how we define the nature of social crisis. It is no longer credible to argue that rising illegitimacy, random violence, and declining values are rooted in either the lack of economic equality or the lack of economic opportunity. These positions are still current in our political debate, but they have lost their root in reality. America's cultural decay can be traced directly to the breakdown of certain institutions—families, churches, neighborhoods, voluntary associations—that act as an immune system against cultural disease. In nearly every community, these institutions once created an atmosphere in which most problems—a teenage girl "in trouble," the rowdy neighborhood kids, the start of a drug problem at the local high school—could be confronted before their repetition threatened the existence of the community itself.

When civil society is strong, it infuses a community with its warmth, trains its people to be good citizens, and transmits values between generations. When it is weak, no amount of police or politics can provide a substitute. There is a growing consensus that a declining civil society undermines both civility and society.

It is, however, the fate of every great and elegant idea to fall into the grubby hands of politicians. The discussion of civil society is not, by definition, primarily political. But it has profound political implications, and predictably, there is the beginning of a struggle for political ownership of these powerful themes. Just as predictably, political uses and abuses of civil society are born of the struggle. There is a strong temptation to insert these ideas into existing political ideologies. But they do not neatly fit. And when forced, the ideas themselves become distorted.

We are now seeing the emerging outlines of an important argument. On one side are "civil society pessimists," often on the left. They understand the destructive decline of family life and civic engagement. But this becomes an excuse for new and varied government roles. Since the family has failed, they argue that enlightened and properly unionized schools must take up the slack, dispensing personal advice and contraceptives. Since citizenship is weak, they think that Americorps is inevitable.

On the other side are the "civil society optimists," often on the right. They seem confident that the retreat of government will *automatically* result in the rebirth of broken families and decimated communities. Civil society is prescribed as an easy, all-purpose antidote to what ails America, allowing Republicans to cut social spending without doubts or nightmares.

Is the decline of mediating structures an excuse for government paternalism? Is the promise of civil society a justification for libertarianism? Neither option seems adequate, and both ring false to our own experience. It is not true that government can replace civic institutions, or that those institutions are hopelessly and permanently feeble. We have seen the healing power of true compassion and spiritual hope, particularly in faith-based charities. Problems that would seem to require an army of social workers and a division of the national guard are solved by love without illusions and without limits. These institutions are the only force in our society that can transform men and women from the soul outward. They are the only force that can turn an addict into an example . . . a troublemaker into a peacemaker . . . a criminal into a man or woman of conscience. And they make every political goal—every New Deal, New Frontier, and New Covenant—look small in comparison.

But it *is* true that, in some communities, the retreat of government will certainly lead to suffering and social dislocation. These consequences may be unintended but they are predictable. As John DiIulio has observed, if a victim is stabbed, you need to remove the knife. But removing the knife will not heal the person. Without some compassionate provision in this period of adjustment, we will end up as Social Darwinists by default.

This leads us to an unavoidable position—what might be termed "civil society realism." The state clearly cannot directly rebuild the institutions of civil society. Using government to recreate community and family, says Don Eberly, is like believing that the "trees move the wind." Yet, particularly in some communities, we must find ways to encourage our civil society to renew itself, despite the difficulty. The alternative is a destructive indifference to human suffering.

This has been the tension inherent in the political arena, as many legislators are attempting to translate some of these ideas into law. There is no government plan to reconstruct our civic life. The state must accept a more limited and humble role. But that role does exist. We have set out to build a positive preference for intact families in our laws. We have proposed ways to replace a significant portion of public welfare with private charity. And we have tried to take the side of people and institutions who are rebuilding their own neighborhoods, and who often feel isolated and poorly equipped. The goal, in the margin where that is possible, is to send America's value-shaping institutions into battle with sufficient resources to reclaim our culture. These proposals were inspired by the challenge set down by Father Richard John Neuhaus and Peter Berger in a slim volume, originally published in 1977 (and recently updated), called *To Empower People*. In that influential book, Neuhaus and Berger wrote about the "value-generating and value-maintaining agencies in society," and they concluded, "If they could be more imaginatively recognized in public policy, individuals would be more 'at home' in society, and the political order would be more meaningful."

The centerpiece of our plan is a charity tax credit. It would allow every taxpaying family to give a portion of what it owes the government each year to private charities in its own communities, including those that are religiously based. To be eligible for such donations, organizations must have as their primary purpose the prevention or alleviation of poverty and must ensure that a certain share—perhaps 75 percent—of their expenses is devoted to poverty programs. The charitable tax credit would be a meaningful alternative to increasing the budgets of federal and state bureaucracies. Who would not prefer giving money to the Salvation Army instead of to HHS? To Habitat for Humanity instead of HUD? To Big Brothers instead of to Big Government? The fatal flaw in government programs is in sterile, valueless bureaucracies themselves. It will take a bold conservatism to adopt the bold dream of breaking the monopoly of government as a provider of compassion and returning its resources to individuals, churches, and charities. Our goal should eventually be not just welfare reform, but welfare replacement.

Education, too, is a vital part of making communities work. To be capable of self-rule, citizens must possess the means and the inclination to participate in public life. This assumes a minimum level of education so that citizens can not only succeed economically and participate meaningfully in public life, but also realize a commonality and cohesion with fellow citizens. Alarm has set in at many public schools in our poorer communities precisely because their students are not achieving this level of skill. School choice offers hope and opportunity to these communities. Through "opportunity scholarships," we can give many low-income families the chance to send their children to those public, private, or parochial schools that succeed in educating and nurturing students from all economic backgrounds. The government can, and should, interject marketplace competition into the public education monopoly so that children, whether rich or poor, may have access to the tools of citizenship.

Similarly, an effective program of economic empowerment in the poorer sections of our urban areas can cultivate those qualities of commitment, association, duty, and pride which, in turn, help to cultivate healthy, sustainable communities. Through the establishment of dozens of "renewal communities" residents can benefit from pro-growth tax incentives and regulatory relief and turn their neighborhoods around. By encouraging homeownership and new business development in our inner cities, we can help spur a renaissance in places that many had written off as unlivable.

Although the most important civic renewal in our nation will take place entirely outside government, in the next few years, a debate will be joined in earnest. How can we reverse the civic and political atrophy of the past thirty years? How can we revive what one scholar calls "institutions that can survive the chaos"? These are the most exciting, important questions of social policy. And the debate itself has already accomplished two very healthy things: first, it has restored to us an understanding of and respect for the complexity of our social crisis. Civil society is organic, not mechanical. It can be coaxed and nurtured, not engineered. It will not be rebuilt by government. Nor will it be rebuilt by "no government." But it must be encouraged to rebuild itself. This is a challenge to our creativity and compassion.

Second, the discussion of civil society has returned hope to our political life. Bob Woodson, executive director of the National Center for Neighborhood Enterprise, has commented that every social problem that threatens our country is being solved . . . somewhere . . . right now . . . by neighborhood healers, armed with spiritual renewal and true compassion. These healers prove that our challenges are not an endless road or a hopeless maze. In an era of "compassion fatigue," they are conducting a war on poverty that marches from victory to victory. Their example offers our nation much-needed encouragement that gives this important movement a direct political appeal. For no lasting political realignment can occur without an element of vision and hope—a message that our worst social problems, while persistent, are not permanent. Hope is what turns a sociological debate into a compelling political theme.

If one of the first responsibilities of a democratic government is to protect the liberty of its people, it then follows that that same government should help sustain the culture and community on which liberty depends. We know where hope is kindled—among individuals and groups engaged in the hard, noble work of restoration. Their victories are among America's great untold stories. No alternative approach to our cultural crisis holds as much promise of these "little platoons," precisely because they have qualities not found in government at any level—spiritual renewal and authentic compassion. As a matter of public policy, and as a matter of prudent politics, it is time to aggressively take their side in the battle to recivilize American society.

16

America's Challenge
Revitalizing Our National Community

BILL BRADLEY

NEVER IN American history has a new vision begun in Washington. Never has it been the sole property of either political party. In fact, to initiate a frank discussion of our current American condition requires us to throw off many of the barnacle-encrusted categories with which we are accustomed to talking about this nation's problems. This could seriously disrupt the respective moral allegiances and political turfs of both the Democratic and Republican parties. I would like to start making that disruption happen, for out of such ferment might emerge the fresh ideas of a better American future.

Our contemporary political debate has settled into two painfully familiar ruts. Republicans, infatuated with the magic of the "private sector," reflexively criticize government as the enemy of freedom. According to their mantra, human needs and the common good are best served through the marketplace.

Democrats tend to distrust the market, seeing it as synonymous with greed and exploitation. Ever confident in the powers of government to solve problems, Democrats instinctively turn to the bureaucratic state to regulate the economy and to solve social problems. Democrats generally prefer the bureaucrat they know to the consumer they can't control. Of course, both parties are somewhat disingenuous. Neither is above making self-serving exceptions. For example, Republicans say they are for the market, but they support market-distorting tax loopholes and wasteful subsidies for special interests as diverse as water, wheat, and wine. Then there are the Democrats who say that they want an activist government but won't raise the taxes to fund it or describe clearly its limits or its necessity. Still, these twin poles of political debate—crudely put, government action versus the free market—dominate our sense of the possible, our sense of what is relevant and meaningful in public affairs. Yet, the issues that most concern Americans today—the plague of violence, guns, and drugs; racial tensions; the turmoil in public education; the deterioration of America's families—seem to have little direct connection with either the market or government.

And in fact, neither government nor the market is equipped to solve America's central problems: the deterioration of our civil society and the need to revitalize our democratic process.

Americans at Home

Civil society is the place where Americans make their home, sustain their marriages, raise their families, hang out with their friends, meet their neighbors, educate their children, worship their god. It is in the churches, schools, fraternities, community centers, labor unions, synagogues, sports leagues, PTAs, libraries, and barber shops. It is where opinions are expressed and refined, where views are exchanged and agreements made, where a sense of common purpose and consensus are forged. It lies apart from the realms of the market and the government, and possesses a different ethic. The market is governed by the logic of economic self-interest, while government is the domain of laws with all their coercive authority. Civil society, on the other hand, is the sphere of our most basic humanity—the personal, everyday realm that is governed by values such as responsibility, trust, fraternity, solidarity, and love. In a democratic civil society such as ours, we also put a special premium on social equality—the conviction that men and women should be measured by the quality of their character and not the color of their skin, the shape of their eyes, the size of their bank account, the religion of their family, or the happenstance of their gender.

What both Democrats and Republicans fail to see is that the government and the market are not enough to make a civilization. There must also be a healthy, robust civic sector—a space in which the bonds of community can flourish. Government and the market are similar to two legs on a three-legged stool. Without the third leg of civil society, the stool is not stable and cannot provide support for a vital America.

Today, however, associations in America seem imperiled. For example, PTA participation has fallen. So have the number of Boy Scouts and Red Cross volunteers. So have labor unions and civic clubs such as the Lions and the Elks. All across America, people are choosing not to join with one another in communal activities. One recent college graduate even volunteered sadly that her suburban Philadelphia neighbors "don't even wave."

Every day the news brings another account of Americans being disconnected from each other. Sometimes the stories, such as that of the married couple in Rochester, New York, who unexpectedly ran into one another on the same airplane as they departed for separate business trips and discovered that each had, unbeknownst to the other, hired a different babysitter to care for their young daughter. Other stories are untinged by comedy, such as that of the suburban Chicago couple who, unbeknownst to their indifferent neighbors, left their two little girls home alone while they vacationed in Mexico. It is tempting to dismiss these stories as isolated cases. But I think they have a grip on our imaginations precisely because they speak to our real fears. They are ugly reminders of the erosion of love, trust, and mutual obligation. They are testimony to a profound human disconnectedness that cuts across most conventional lines of class, race, and geography.

That is one reason, perhaps, that we used to love the television show *Cheers*. It is the bar "where everyone knows your name." How many of us are blessed with such a place in our lives? How many of us know the names, much less the life stories of all the neighbors in our section of town or even on several floors of our apartment building?

To the sophisticates of national politics, it all sounds too painfully small time, even corny to focus on these things. After all, voluntary local associations and community connection seem so peripheral to both the market and government; both the market and the government have far more raw power. Government and business are national and international in scope. They're on TV. They talk casually about billions of dollars. In many ways the worlds of politics and business have de-legitimized the local, the social, the cultural, the spiritual. Yet upon these things lies the whole edifice of our national well-being.

Strengthening Citizenship

Alongside the decline of civil society is a sad truth that the exercise of democratic citizenship plays, at best, a very minor role in the lives of most American adults. Only 39 percent of the eligible voters actually voted in 1994. The role formerly played by party organizations with face to face associations has been yielded to the media, where local TV news follows the dual credos, "If it bleeds, it leads, and if it thinks, it stinks," and paid media politics remains beyond the reach of most Americans. When only the rich, such as Ross Perot, can get their views across on TV, political equality suffers. The rich have a loudspeaker and everyone else gets a megaphone. Make no mistake about it, money talks in American politics today as never before, and no revival of our democratic culture can occur until citizens feel that their participation is more meaningful than the money lavished by PACs and big donors.

Then there are the political campaigns that short-circuit deliberative judgment. People sit at home as spectators, wait to be entertained in thirty-second prepolled, pretested emotional appeals and then render a thumbs up or a thumbs down almost on a whim. From the Long House of the Iroquois to the general store of de Tocqueville's America to the Chautauquas of the late nineteenth century, to the Jaycees, Lions, parent-teacher associations, and political clubs of the early 1960s, Americans have always had places where they could come together and deliberate about their common future. Today there are fewer and fewer forums where people actually listen to one another. It's as if everyone wants to spout his opinion or her criticism and then moves on.

So what does all this imply for public policy?

First, we need to strengthen the crucible of civil society, the American family. Given the startling increase in the number of children growing up with one parent and paltry resources, we need to recouple sex and parental responsibility by holding men accountable for sexual irresponsibility. Policy should send a very clear message—if you have sex with someone and she becomes pregnant, be prepared to have 15 percent of your wages for eighteen years go to support the mother and child. Fatherhood is a lifetime commitment that takes time and money.

And, given that 40 percent of American children now live in homes where both parents work, we have only four options if we believe our rhetoric about the importance of child-rearing: higher compensation for one spouse so that the other can stay home permanently; a loving relative in the neighborhood; more taxes or higher salaries to pay for more daycare programs; or, parental leave measured in years, not weeks, and available for a mother and a father at different times in a career. The only given is that someone has to care for the children.

Second, we need to create more quality civic space. The most underutilized resource in most of our communities is the public school, which too often closes at 4:00 p.m. only to see children in suburbs return to empty homes with television as their babysitter or, in cities, to the street corners where gangs make them an offer they can't refuse. Keeping the schools open on weekdays after hours, and on weekends, with supervision coming from the community, would give some kids a place to study until their parents picked them up or at least would provide a safe haven from the war zone outside.

Third, we need a more civic-minded media. At a time when harassed parents spend less time with their children, they have ceded to television more and more of the all-important role of storytelling, which is essential to the formation of moral education that sustains a civil society. But too often TV producers and music executives and video game manufacturers feed young people a menu of violence without context and sex without attachment, and both with no consequences or judgment. The market acts blindly to sell and to make money, never pausing to ask whether it furthers citizenship or decency. Too often those who trash government as the enemy of freedom and a destroyer of families are strangely silent about the market's corrosive effects on those very same values in civil society. The answer is not censorship, but more citizenship in the corporate boardroom and more active families who will turn off the trash, boycott the sponsors, and tell the executives that you hold them personally responsible for making money from glorifying violence and human degradation.

Fourth, in an effort to revitalize the democratic process, we have to take financing of elections out of the hands of the special interests and turn it over to the people by taking two simple steps. Allow taxpayers to check off on their tax returns above their tax liability up to $200 for political campaigns for federal office in their state. Before the general election, divide the fund between Democrat, Republican, or qualified independent candidates. No other money would be legal—no PACs, no bundles, no big contributions, no party conduits—even the bankroll of a millionaire candidate would be off-limits. If the people of a state choose to give little, then they will be less informed, but this would be the citizen's choice. If there were less money involved, the process would adjust. Who knows, maybe attack ads would go and public discourse would grow.

The Language of Civil Society

Public policy, as these suggestions illustrate, can help facilitate the revitalization of democracy and civil society, but it cannot create civil society. We can insist that fathers support their children financially, but fathers have to see the importance of spending time with their children. We can figure out ways, such as parental leave, to provide parents with more time with their children, but parents have to use that time to raise their children. We can create community schools, but communities have to use them. We can provide mothers and fathers with the tools they need to influence the storytelling of the mass media, but they ultimately must exercise that control. We can take special interests out of elections, but only people can vote. We can provide opportunities for a more deliberative citizenship at both the national and the local level, but citizens have to seize those opportunities and take individual responsibility.

One way to encourage such responsibility is to give the distinctive moral language of civil society a more permanent place in our public conversation. The language of the marketplace says, "get as much as you can for yourself." The language of government says, "legislate for others what is good for them." But the language of community, family, and citizenship at its core is about receiving undeserved gifts. What this nation needs to promote is the spirit of giving something freely, without measuring it out precisely or demanding something in return.

At a minimum that language has to be given equal time with the language of rights that dominates our culture. Rights talk properly supports an individual's status and dignity within a community. It has done much to protect the less powerful in our society and should not be abandoned. The problem comes in the adversarial dynamic that rights talk sets up in which people assert themselves through confrontation, championing one right to the exclusion of another. Instead of working together to improve our collective situation, we fight with each other over who has superior rights. Americans are too often given to speaking of America as a country in which you have the right to do whatever you want. On reflection, most of us will admit that no country could long survive that lived by such a principle. And this talk is deeply at odds with the best interests of civil society.

Forrest Gump and Rush Limbaugh were the surprise stars of the first half of the 1990s because they poked fun at hypocrisy and the inadequacy of what we have today. But they are not builders. The builders are those in localities across America who are constructing bridges of cooperation and dialogue in face to face meetings with their supporters and their adversaries. Alarmed at the decline of civil society, they know how to understand the legitimate point of view of those with whom they disagree. In Washington, action too often surrounds only competition for power. With the media's help, words are used to polarize and to destroy people. In cities across America where citizens are working together, words are tools to build bridges between people. For example, at New Communities Corporation in Newark, New Jersey, people are too busy doing things to spend energy figuring out how to tear down. In these places there are more barn-raisers than barn-burners. Connecting their idealism with national policy offers us our greatest hope and our biggest challenge.

Above all, we need to understand that a true civil society in which citizens interact on a regular basis to grapple with common problems will not occur because of the arrival of a hero. Rebuilding civil society requires people talking and listening to each other, not blindly following a hero.

I was reminded a few years ago of the temptation offered by the "knight in shining armor" when the cover of a national magazine had Gen. Colin Powell's picture on it with a caption something like "Will he be the answer to our problems?" If the problem is a deteriorating civic culture, then a charismatic leader, be he the president or a general, is not the answer. He or she might make us feel better momentarily, but then if we are only spectators thrilled by the performance, how have we progressed collectively? A character in Bertolt Brecht's *Galileo* says "Pity the nation that has no heroes," to which Galileo responds, "Pity the nation that needs them." All of us have to go out in the public square and all of us have to assume our citizenship responsibilities. In a vibrant civil society, real leadership at the top is made possible by the understanding and evolution of leaders of awareness at the bottom and in the middle, that is, citizens engaged in a deliberative discussion about our common future. The more open our public dialogue, the larger the number of Americans who join our deliberation, the greater the chance we have to build a better country and a better world.

PART THREE

Philosophical Responses

17

Second Thoughts on Civil Society

GERTRUDE HIMMELFARB

I WOULD LIKE to think that it is not just contrariness on my part that makes me wince, these days, on hearing talk of civil society. Liberals and conservatives, communitarians and libertarians, Democrats and Republicans, academics and politicians appeal to civil society as the remedy for our dire condition. They agree upon little else but this, that mediating structures, voluntary associations, families, communities, churches, and workplaces are the corrective to an inordinate individualism and an overweening state.

The ubiquity of the phrase is enough to make it suspect. What can it mean if people of such diverse views can invoke it so enthusiastically? I am as critical as anyone (perhaps more than most) of an individualism that is self-absorbed and self-indulgent, obsessively concerned with the rights, liberties, and choices of the "autonomous" person. And I am no less critical of a state that has usurped the authority of those institutions in civil society which once mitigated that excessive individualism. But I am also wary of civil society used as a rhetorical panacea, as if the mere invocation of the term is a solution to all problems—an easy, painless solution, a happy compromise between two extremes.

Civil society is indeed in a sorry condition. The welfare state is a classic case of the appropriation by government of the functions traditionally performed by families and localities. Neighbors feel no obligation to help one another when they can call upon the government for assistance. Private and religious charities are often little more than conduits of the state for the distribution of public funds (and are obliged to distribute those funds in accord with the requirements fixed by government bureaucrats).

But it is not only the weakness of civil society that is at fault. Some of the institutions of civil society—private schools and universities, unions, and nonprofit foundations, civic and cultural organizations—are stronger and more influential than ever. And they have been complicitous in fostering the very evils that civil society is supposed to mitigate. The individualistic ideology of rights and the statist ideology of big government are reflected in the causes that these institutions have promoted: feminism, multiculturalism, affirmative action, political correctness.

Proponents of civil society try to rescue the concept by specifying that the mediating structures they are talking about are not these large, bureaucratic quasi-public institutions, but small, voluntary, face-to-face groups. But these too are sometimes part of the problem rather than the solution. The family, the most basic and intimate unit of civil society, is hardly a paragon of virtue. For a long time social workers, committed to the family as the natural, proper habitat for the child, made every effort to keep abused children with their abusive parents. Only recently, confronted with cases of the most flagrant cruelty, have some of them been persuaded to remove those children from their "dysfunctional families," as the euphemism has it.

Nor is the face-to-face principle reliable in other instances. It is instructive to recall that a great impetus to the ideology of absolute individual rights and freedom of choice came from small, neighborly face-to-face groups in the early 1970s—the consciousness-raising sessions that heralded the feminist movement. Today, we have other face-to-face groups—neighborhood gangs, for example—that by this definition qualify as members of civil society but are hardly what the proponents of civil society have in mind.

What is required, then, is not only a restoration of civil society but the far more difficult task of reformation—moral reformation. Even to articulate the problem is difficult, because the language of morality has become suspect. One of the reasons the idea of civil society is so attractive is that it is couched in the language of sociology, which speaks of society in structural and functional terms. In ordinary times, that language is sufficient for purposes of analysis and reform, because underlying those structures and functions is a moral consensus that is taken for granted, values that may not be articulated but that are the bedrock of society. It is only when the consensus is shattered that we are driven to reexamine those values to try to understand why our mediating structures have failed.

The sociological mode is also congenial because it conforms to the relativistic temper of our time. Structures and functions are malleable; they may take one form or another depending upon time, place, and circumstance. Sociologists have assured us that the "breakdown" (in quotation marks) of the family is nothing more than the replacement of the "nuclear," "bourgeois" family by new forms performing the same function: single-parent families, or families consisting of stepparents, grandparents, "cohabitors," or (the latest variant on this theory) "pure relationships" of friends who assume the role and function of kin.

This capacious view of the family has been shaken recently by a substantial body of empirical evidence demonstrating that not all families are structurally and functionally equivalent, that some forms (the fatherless family, most notably) are more inclined than others to be "dysfunctional," contributing to the "social pathology" of crime, violence, illegitimacy, illiteracy, welfare dependency, and the like. Even now, however, we shy away from the language of morality. We speak of the "dysfunctional" family as if the problem is only functional, or of "social" pathology, as if society is at fault for these ills, or "alternative lifestyles," as if they are true alternatives and mere styles.

It is because we cannot face up to the moral nature of the problem that we look for solutions that are at best irrelevant and sometimes counterproductive. Take the efforts being made to force deadbeat fathers to meet their child-support payments. On the face of it, such measures seem eminently fair and sensible. Surely, the father should assume financial responsibility for his children and help the hard-pressed mother stay off the relief rolls. But money itself is not the problem; the real problem is the absence of the father. And that problem may actually be aggravated if these measures succeed, for the absent father will feel that he has met his obligations by making those payments, and the single mother, assured of a regular income, will feel free to enter into the most casual relationships and have children without any commitment of marriage. The cash-nexus, as Marxists used to say, is not a viable basis for society—certainly not a viable basis for the family.

Or compare the best-intentioned divorced father today with the typical immigrant father a generation or two ago (or some immigrant fathers today). The divorced father may make a sincere effort to give "quality time" to his children, spend the occasional weekend with them, take them to a ballgame, and attend their school plays. The immigrant father, on the other hand, leaving for work early in the morning and returning late in the evening had no time to play with his children or share in their activities, and in any case could not have done so because of the cultural gap. Yet he was the better father, one suspects, because he was a permanent, reliable, secure presence in the household—a moral presence whose commitment to his family was unqualified and unproblematic.

When we speak of the breakdown of the family, it is a moral breakdown we are talking about. And when we speak of the restoration of civil society, it is a moral restoration we should seek. That restoration may actually take us outside the realm of civil society, for the mediating structures of civil society are themselves dependent on the well-being of the individuals who participate in them and of the state that protects and legitimizes them.

It is the individual, after all, who is called upon to be a good mother or father, a considerate neighbor, and responsible citizen. The devolution, for example, of welfare to state and local governments is only superficially a structural reform. The objective is the reform of the recipients of welfare by fostering those virtues—work, diligence, self-reliance, self-discipline—that make for more responsible individuals and better members of civil society. Similarly, tax deductions for charitable contributions are meant not only to increase the amount of money donated to charity but also to encourage the virtue of charity, to bring out what the Victorian philosopher T. H. Green called the "best self" of the individual.

If the individual requires "remoralization," so does the state. It is often said that one cannot legislate morality. Yet we have done just that. Civil rights legislation has succeeded in illegitimizing racist conduct, morally as well as legally. Or a welfare system that subsidizes illegitimacy implicitly legitimizes it. Or a school that distributes condoms legitimizes promiscuity. Or a "no fault" divorce code, by destigmatizing divorce, legitimizes it. Or a court decision that disallows the posting of the Ten Commandments in a public school or prayer on a public occasion illegitimizes the public expression of religious beliefs and sentiments.

For good or bad, the state is as much the repository and transmitter of values as are the institutions of civil society. Legislation, judicial decisions, administrative regulations, educational requirements, the tax codes are all instruments of legitimization—or illegitimization. The appeal to civil society is a salutary corrective to big government but should not be taken as an invitation to demean government itself. Especially at this time, when so many traditional institutions are being undermined, we should be wary of the subversion of our political institutions. Moreover, it is just now that we have need of all the resources available to us—public and private, secular and religious, governmental and civic. Edmund Burke's "little platoons" has become the slogan of civil society. But Burke also paid tribute to the state as "a partnership in all science; a partnership in all art; a partnership in every virtue, and in all perfection." We often have good reason to deplore that partnership, but we cannot deny it or ignore it.

By all means, then, let us restore and reform civil society. But let it be a tougher civil society than that envisaged by many who speak in its name. The recent debate on welfare, suggesting that private charities assume a greater responsibility for relief, may have contributed to a softer view of civil society by identifying it with the "caring" or "nurturing" virtues: compassion, tolerance, generosity, benevolence. But there is another set of virtues traditionally promoted by civil society, the "vigorous" virtues, as Shirley Letwin, the biographer of Lady Thatcher, calls them: adventurousness, energy, independence, courage.

The two are not incompatible. It was Margaret Thatcher, herself a vigorous proponent of those virtues, who revived the idea of "Victorian virtues"(or "Victorian values," as the term was corrupted by reporters), recalling a period when both orders of virtues coexisted happily. The great entrepreneurs of the Victorian age were also the great philanthropists. Self-help and helping others were two sides of the same coin. "We have to use charity," said the secretary of the Charity Organisation Society, "to create the powers of self-help." Samuel Smiles, author of the bestseller, *Self-Help*, also wrote a book entitled *Duty* extolling that other Victorian virtue, responsibility to others.

If civil society is to promote the vigorous as well as the nurturing virtues, it has to be vigorous in pursuit of both. That vigor is notably lacking among many of its present advocates, who think that by calling for a restoration of civil society, they are absolved of making those hard choices that will actually restrain the excesses of individualism and statism. For some, civil society has become little more than a surrogate for the state charged with doing everything the state is currently doing; it is the welfare state "with a human face." Others (sometimes the same people) assure us that civil society need not infringe on individual rights and the freedom of choice; it can curb pornography without resorting to anything like censorship, or criminality without any diminution of civil liberties (or what has come to be regarded as such), or the breakdown of the family without any restrictions on divorce or any prejudice against alternative lifestyles. It is also remarkable how often civil society is invoked without any reference to one of its most important institutions, the churches; having driven religion out of the public square, many proponents of civil society would also like to see it removed from that semipublic square known as civil society.

Above all, what is generally lacking in the discussion of civil society is any reference to morality and moral sanctions; instead we are more likely to be warned against any display of "moralism" and "judgmentalism." We are permitted to acclaim charity, compassion, and neighborliness as virtues, but not to "stigmatize" illegitimacy, promiscuity, or chronic dependency as vices. And they may not be stigmatized either by word or deed—by language suggesting that they are discreditable or policies that deem them unworthy of public support.

Yet this is precisely the function of civil society: to encourage moral behavior and discourage—which is to say, stigmatize—immoral behavior. The mechanisms of approbation and disapprobation are all the more necessary in a liberal society, for the more effective the social sanctions, the less need there is for the legal and penal sanctions of the state. If the advocates of civil society are serious in their desire to mediate between the individual and the state, they have to endow civil society with the authority to do so. They have to be as candid in censuring vice as they are in applauding virtue. They have to restore not only institutions of civil society but the force of social and moral suasion. Only then will civil society be what Tocqueville took it to be: the essential constituent of a liberal and democratic society.

18

The Idea of Civil Society

A Path to Social Reconstruction

MICHAEL WALZER

MY AIM in this essay is to defend a complex, imprecise, and, at crucial points, uncertain account of society and politics. I have no hope of theoretical simplicity, not at this historical moment when so many stable oppositions of political and intellectual life have collapsed; but I also have no desire for simplicity, since a world that theory could fully grasp and neatly explain would not, I suspect, be a pleasant place. In the nature of things, then, my argument won't be elegant, and though I believe that arguments should march, the sentences following one another like soldiers on parade, the route of my march today will be twisting and roundabout. I shall begin with the idea of civil society, recently revived by central and east European intellectuals, and go on to talk about the state, the economy, and the nation, and then about civil society and the state again. These are the crucial social formations that we inhabit, but we don't at this moment live comfortably in any of them. Nor is it possible to imagine, in accordance with one or another of the great simplifying theories, a way to choose among them—as if we were destined to find, one day, the best social formation. I mean to argue against choosing, but I shall also claim that it is from within civil society that this argument is best understood.

The words "civil society" name the space of uncoerced human association and also the set of relational networks—formed for the sake of family, faith, interest, and ideology—that fill this space. Central and east European dissidence flourished within a highly restricted version of civil society, and the first task of the new democracies created by the dissidents, so we are told, is to rebuild the networks: unions, churches, political parties and movements, cooperatives, neighborhoods, schools of thought, societies for promoting or preventing this or that. In the West, by contrast, we have lived in civil society for many years without knowing it. Or, better, since the Scottish Enlightenment, or since Hegel, the words have been known to the knowers of such things but they have rarely served to focus anyone else's attention. Now writers in Hungary, Czechoslovakia, and Poland invite us to think about how this social formation is secured and invigorated.

We have reasons of our own for accepting the invitation. Increasingly, associational life in the "advanced" capitalist and social democratic countries seems at risk. Publicists and preachers warn us of a steady attenuation of everyday cooperation and civic friendship. And this time it's possible that they are not, as they usually are, foolishly alarmist. Our cities really are noisier and nastier than they once were. Other people, strangers on the street, seem less trustworthy than they once were. The Hobbesian account of society is more persuasive than it once was.

Perhaps this worrisome picture follows—in part, no more, but what else can a political theorist say? — from the fact that we have not thought enough about solidarity and trust or planned for their future. We have been thinking too much about social formations different from, in competition with, civil society. And so we have neglected the networks through which civility is produced and reproduced. Imagine that the following questions were posed one or two centuries ago to political theorists and moral philosophers: what is the preferred setting, the most supportive environment, for the good life? What sorts of institutions should we work for? Nineteenth- and twentieth-century social thought provides four different, by now familiar, answers to these questions. Think of them as four rival ideologies, each with its own claim to completeness and correctness. Each is importantly wrong. Each neglects the necessary pluralism of any civil society. Each is predicated on an assumption I mean to attack: that such questions must receive a singular answer.

Definitions from the Left

I shall begin, since this is for me the best-known ground, with two leftist answers. The first of the two holds that the preferred setting for the good life is the political community, the democratic state, within which we can be citizens: freely engaged, fully committed, decisionmaking members. And a citizen, on this view, is much the best thing to be. To live well is to be politically active, working with our fellow citizens, collectively determining our common destiny—not for the sake of this or that determination but for the work itself, in which our highest capacities as rational and moral agents find expression. We know ourselves best as persons who propose, debate, and decide.

This argument goes back to the Greeks, but we are most likely to recognize its neoclassical versions. It is Rousseau's argument, or the standard leftist interpretation of Rousseau's argument. His understanding of citizenship as moral agency is one of the key sources of democratic idealism. We can see it at work in a liberal such as John Stuart Mill, in whose writings it produced an unexpected defense of syndicalism (what is today called "workers' control") and, more generally, of social democracy. It appeared among nineteenth- and twentieth-century democratic radicals, often with a hard populist edge. It played a part in the reiterated demand for social inclusion by women, workers, blacks, and new immigrants, all of whom based their claims on their capacity as agents. And this same neoclassical idea of citizenship resurfaced in the 1960s in New Left theories of participation, where it was, however, like latter-day revivals of many ideas, highly theoretical and without much local resonance.

Today, perhaps in response to the political disasters of the late 1960s, "communitarians" in the United States struggle to give Rousseauian idealism a historical reference, looking back to the early American republic and calling for a renewal of civic virtue. They prescribe citizenship as an antidote to the fragmentation of contemporary society—for these theorists, like Rousseau, are disinclined to value the fragments. In their hands, republicanism is still a simplifying creed. If politics is our highest calling, then we are called away from every other activity (or, every other activity is redefined in political terms); our energies are directed toward policy formation and decisionmaking in the democratic state.

I don't doubt that the active and engaged citizen is an attractive figure—even if some of the activists that we actually meet carrying placards and shouting slogans aren't all that attractive. The most penetrating criticism of this first answer to the question about the good life is not that the life isn't good but that it isn't the "real life" of very many people in the modern world. This is so in two senses. First, though the power of the democratic state has grown enormously, partly (and rightly) in response to the demands of engaged citizens, it can't be said that the state is fully in the hands of its citizens. And the larger it gets, the more it takes over those smaller associations still subject to hands-on control. The rule of the demos is in significant ways illusory; the participation of ordinary men and women in the activities of the state (unless they are state employees) is largely vicarious; even party militants are more likely to argue and complain than actually to decide.

Second, despite the singlemindedness of republican ideology, politics rarely engages the full attention of the citizens who are supposed to be its chief protagonists. They have too many other things to worry about. Above all, they have to earn a living. They are more deeply engaged in the economy than in the political community. Republican theorists (like Hannah Arendt) recognized this engagement only as a threat to civic virtue. Economic activity belongs to the realm of necessity, they argue, politics to the realm of freedom. Ideally, citizens should not have to work; they should be served by machines, if not by slaves, so that they can flock to the assemblies and argue with their fellows about affairs of state. In practice, however, work, though it begins in necessity, takes on a value of its own—expressed in commitment to a career, pride in a job well done, a sense of camaraderie in the workplace. All of these are competitive with the values of citizenship.

The second leftist position on the preferred setting for the good life involves a turning away from republican politics and a focus instead on economic activity. We can think of this as the socialist answer to the questions I began with; it can be found in Marx and also, though the arguments are somewhat different, among the utopians he hoped to supersede. For Marx, the preferred setting is the cooperative economy, where we can all be producers—artists (Marx was a romantic), inventors, and artisans. (Assembly line workers don't quite seem to fit.) This again is much the best thing to be. The picture Marx paints is of creative men and women making useful and beautiful objects, not for the sake of this or that object but for the sake of creativity itself, the highest expression of our "species-being" as *homo faber*, man-the-maker.

The state, in this view, ought to be managed in such a way as to set productivity free. It doesn't matter who the managers are so long as they are committed to this goal and rational in its pursuit. Their work is technically important but not substantively interesting. Once productivity is free, politics simply ceases to engage anyone's attention. Before that time, in the Marxist here and now, political conflict is taken to be the superstructural enactment of economic conflict, and democracy is valued mainly because it enables socialist movements and parties to organize for victory. The value is instrumental and historically specific. A democratic state is the preferred setting not for the good life but for the class struggle: the purpose of the struggle is to win, and victory brings an end to democratic instrumentality. There is no intrinsic value in democracy, no reason to think that politics has, for creatures like us, a permanent attractiveness. When we are all engaged in productive activity, social division and the conflicts it engenders will disappear, and the state, in the once-famous phrase, will "wither away."

In fact, if this vision were ever realized, it is politics that would wither away. Some kind of administrative agency would still be necessary for economic coordination, and it is only a Marxist conceit to refuse to call this agency a state. "Society regulates the general production," Marx wrote in *The German Ideology*, "and thus makes it possible for me to do one thing today and another tomorrow . . . just as I have a mind." Because this regulation is nonpolitical, the individual producers are freed from the burdens of citizenship. They attend instead to the things they make and to the cooperative relationships they establish. Exactly how one can work with other people and still do whatever one pleases is unclear to me and probably to most readers of Marx. The texts suggest an extraordinary faith in the virtuosity of the regulators. No one, I think, quite shares this faith today, but something like it helps to explain the tendency of some leftists to see even the liberal and democratic state as an obstacle that has to be, in the worst of recent jargons, "smashed."

The seriousness of Marxist antipolitics is nicely illustrated by Marx's own dislike of syndicalism. What the syndicalists proposed was a neat amalgam of the first and second answers to the question about the good life: for them, the preferred setting was the worker-controlled factory, where men and women were simultaneously citizens and producers, making decisions and making things. Marx seems to have regarded the combination as impossible; factories could not be both democratic and productive. This is the point of Engels's little essay on authority, which I take to express Marx's view also. More generally, self-government on the job called into question the legitimacy of "social regulation" or state planning, which alone, Marx thought, could enable individual workers to devote themselves, without distraction, to their work.

But this vision of the cooperative economy is set against an unbelievable background—a nonpolitical state, regulation without conflict, "the administration of things." In every actual experience of socialist politics, the state has moved rapidly into the foreground, and most socialists, in the West at least, have been driven to make their own amalgam of the first and second answers. They call themselves *democratic* socialists, focusing on the state as well as (in fact, much more than) on the economy and doubling the preferred settings for the good life. Because I believe that two are better than one, I take this to be progress. But before I try to suggest what further progress might look like, I need to describe two more ideological answers to the question about the good life, one of them capitalist, the other nationalist. For there is no reason to think that only leftists love singularity.

A Capitalist Definition

The third answer holds that the preferred setting for the good life is the marketplace, where individual men and women, consumers rather than producers, choose among a maximum number of options. The autonomous individual confronting his, and now her, possibilities—this is much the best thing to be. To live well is not to make political decisions or beautiful objects; it is to make personal choices. Not any particular choices, for no choice is substantively the best: it is the activity of choosing that makes for autonomy. And the market within which choices are made, like the socialist economy, largely dispenses with politics; it requires at most a minimal state, no "social regulation," only the police.

Production, too, is free even if it isn't, as in the Marxist vision, freely creative. More important than the producers, however, are the entrepreneurs—heroes of autonomy, consumers of opportunity—who compete to supply whatever all the other consumers want or might be persuaded to want. Entrepreneurial activity tracks consumer preference. Though not without its own excitements, it is mostly instrumentality: the aim of all entrepreneurs (and all producers) is to increase their market power, maximize their options. Competing with one another, they maximize everyone else's options too, filling the marketplace with desirable objects. The market is preferred (over the political community and the cooperative economy) because of its fullness. Freedom, in the capitalist view, is a function of plenitude. We can only choose when we have many choices.

It is also true, unhappily, that we can only make effective (rather than merely speculative or wistful) choices when we have resources to dispose of. But people come to the marketplace with radically unequal resources—some with virtually nothing at all. Not everyone can compete successfully in commodity production, and therefore not everyone has access to commodities. Autonomy turns out to be a high-risk value, which many men and women can only realize with help from their friends. The market, however, is not a good setting for mutual assistance, for I cannot help someone else without reducing (for the short term, at least) my own options. And I have no reason, as an autonomous individual, to accept any reductions of any sort for someone else's sake. My argument here is not that autonomy in the marketplace provides no support for social solidarity. Despite the successes of capitalist production, the good life of consumer choice is not universally available. Large numbers of people drop out of the market economy or live precariously on its margins.

Partly for this reason, capitalism, like socialism, is highly dependent on state action—not only to prevent theft and enforce contracts but also to regulate the economy and guarantee the minimal welfare of its participants. But these participants, insofar as they are market activists, are not active in the state: capitalism in its ideal form, like socialism again, does not make for citizenship. Or, its protagonists conceive of citizenship in economic terms, so that citizens are transformed into autonomous consumers, looking for the party or program that most persuasively promises to strengthen their market positions. They need the state but have no moral relation to it, and they control its officials only as consumers control the producers of commodities, by buying or not buying what they make.

Because the market has no political boundaries, capitalist entrepreneurs also evade official control. They need the state but have no loyalty to it; the profit motive brings them into conflict with democratic regulation. So arms merchants sell the latest military technology to foreign powers, and manufacturers move their factories overseas to escape safety codes or minimum-wage laws. Multinational corporations stand outside (and to some extent against) every political community. They are known only by their brand names, which, unlike family names and country names, evoke preferences but not affections or solidarities.

A Nationalist Response

The fourth answer to the question about the good life can be read as a response to market amorality and disloyalty, though it has, historically, other sources as well. According to the fourth answer, the preferred setting is the nation, within which we are loyal members, bound to one another by ties of blood and history. And a member, secure in membership, literally part of an organic whole—this is much the best thing to be. To live well is to participate with other men and women in remembering, cultivating, and passing on a national heritage. This is so, on the nationalist view, without reference to the specific content of the heritage, so long as it is one's own, a matter of birth, not choice. Every nationalist will, of course, find value in his or her own heritage, but the highest value is not in the finding but in the willing: the firm identification of the individual with a people and a history.

Nationalism has often been a leftist ideology, historically linked to democracy and even to socialism. But it is most characteristically an ideology of the right, for its understanding of membership is ascriptive; it requires no political choices and no activity beyond ritual affirmation. When nations find themselves ruled by foreigners, however, ritual affirmation isn't enough. Then nationalism requires a more heroic loyalty: self-sacrifice in the struggle for national liberation. The capacity of the nation to elicit such sacrifices from its members is proof of the importance of this fourth answer. Individual members seek the good life by seeking autonomy not for themselves but for their people. Ideally, this attitude ought to survive the liberation struggle and provide a foundation for social solidarity and mutual assistance. Perhaps, to some extent, it does: certainly the welfare state has had its greatest successes in ethnically homogeneous countries. It is also true, however, that once liberation has been secured, nationalist men and women are commonly content with a vicarious rather than a practical participation in the community. There is nothing wrong with vicarious participation, on the nationalist view, since the good life is more a matter of identity than activity—faith, not works, so to speak, though both of these are understood in secular terms.

In the modern world, nations commonly seek statehood, for their autonomy will always be at risk if they lack sovereign power. But they don't seek states of any particular kind. No more do they seek economic arrangements of any particular kind. Unlike religious believers who are their close kin and (often) bitter rivals, nationalists are not bound by a body of authoritative law or a set of sacred texts. Beyond liberation, they have no program, only a vague commitment to continue a history, to sustain a "way of life." Their own lives, I suppose, are emotionally intense, but in relation to society and economy this is a dangerously free-floating intensity. In time of trouble, it can readily be turned against other nations, particularly against the internal others: minorities, aliens, strangers. Democratic citizenship, worker solidarity, free enterprise, and consumer autonomy—all these are less exclusive than nationalism but not always resistant to its power. The ease with which citizens, workers, and consumers become fervent nationalists is a sign of the inadequacy of the first three answers to the question about the good life. The nature of nationalist fervor signals the inadequacy of the fourth.

Can We Find a Synthesis?

All these answers are wrongheaded because of their singularity. They miss the complexity of human society, the inevitable conflicts of commitment and loyalty. Hence I am uneasy with the idea that there might be a fifth answer, the newest one (it draws upon less central themes of nineteenth- and twentieth-century social thought), which holds that the good life can only be lived in civil society, the realm of fragmentation and struggle but also of concrete and authentic solidarities, where we fulfill E. M. Forster's injunction, "only connect" and become sociable or communal men and women. And this is, of course, much the best thing to be. The picture here is of people freely associating and communicating with one another, forming and reforming groups of all sorts, not for the sake of any particular formation—family, tribe, nation, religion, commune, brotherhood or sisterhood, interest group or ideological movement—but for the sake of sociability itself. For we are by nature social, before we are political or economic beings.

I would rather say that the civil society argument is a corrective to the four ideological accounts of the good life—part denial, part incorporation—rather than a fifth to stand alongside them. It challenges their singularity but it has no singularity of its own. The phrase "social being" describes men and women who are citizens, producers, consumers, members of the nation, and much else besides—and none of these by nature or because it is the best thing to be. The associational life of civil society is the actual ground where all versions of the good are worked out and tested . . . and proved to be partial, incomplete, ultimately unsatisfying. It can't be the case that living on this ground is good in itself; there isn't any other place to live. What is true is that the quality of our political and economic activity and of our national culture is intimately connected to the strength and vitality of our associations.

Ideally, civil society is a setting of settings: all are included, none is preferred. The argument is a liberal version of the four answers, accepting them all, insisting that each leave room for the others, therefore not finally accepting any of them. Liberalism appears here as an anti-ideology, and this is an attractive position in the contemporary world. I shall stress this attractiveness as I try to explain how civil society might actually incorporate and deny the four answers. Later on, however, I shall have to argue that this position too, so genial and benign, has its problems.

Let's begin with the political community and the cooperative economy, taken together. These two leftist versions of the good life systematically undervalued all associations except the demos and the working class. Their protagonists could imagine conflicts between political communities and between classes but not within either; they aimed at the abolition or transcendence of particularism and all its divisions. Theorists of civil society, by contrast, have a more realistic view of communities and economies. They are more accommodating to conflict—that is, to political opposition and economic competition. Associational freedom serves for them to legitimate a set of market relations, though not necessarily the capitalist set. The market, when it is entangled in the network of associations, when the forms of ownership are pluralized, is without doubt the economic formation most consistent with the civil society argument. This same argument also serves to legitimate a kind of state that is liberal and pluralist more than republican (not so radically dependent upon the virtue of its citizens). Indeed, a state of this sort, as we shall see, is necessary if associations are to flourish.

Once incorporated into civil society, neither citizenship nor production can ever again be all-absorbing. They will have their votaries, but these people will not be models for the rest of us—or, they will be partial models only, for some people at some time of their lives, not for other people, not at other times. This pluralist perspective follows in part, perhaps, from the lost romance of work, from our experience with the new productive technologies and the growth of the service economy. Service is more easily reconciled with a vision of human beings as social animals than with *homo faber*. What can a hospital attendant or a schoolteacher or a marriage counselor or a social worker or a television repairperson or a government official be said to *make*? The contemporary economy does not offer many people a chance for creativity in the Marxist sense. Nor does Marx (or any socialist thinker of the central tradition) have much to say about those men and women whose economic activity consists entirely in helping other people. The helpmate, like the housewife, was never assimilated to the class of workers.

In similar fashion, politics in the contemporary democratic state does not offer many people a chance for Rousseauian self-determination. Citizenship, taken by itself, is today mostly a passive role: citizens are spectators who vote. Between elections they are served, well or badly, by the civil service. They are not at all like those heroes of republican mythology, the citizens of ancient Athens meeting in assembly and (foolishly, as it turned out) deciding to invade Sicily. But in the associational networks of civil society—in unions, parties, movements, interest groups, and so on— these same people make many smaller decisions and shape to some degree the more distant determinations of state and economy. And in a more densely organized, more egalitarian civil society, they might do both these things to greater effect.

These socially engaged men and women—part-time union officers, movement activists, party regulars, consumer advocates, welfare volunteers, church members, family heads—stand outside the republic of citizens as it is commonly conceived. They are only intermittently virtuous; they are too caught up in particularity. They look, most of them, for many partial fulfillments, no longer for the one clinching fulfillment. On the ground of actuality (unless the state usurps the ground), citizenship shades off into a great diversity of (sometimes divisive) decisionmaking roles; and, similarly, production shades off into a multitude of (sometimes competitive) socially useful activities. It is, then, a mistake to set politics and work in opposition to one another. There is no ideal fulfillment and no essential human capacity. We require many settings so that we can live different kinds of good lives.

All this is not to say, however, that we need to accept the capitalist version of competition and division. Theorists who regard the market as the preferred setting for the good life aim to make it the actual setting for as many aspects of life as possible. Their singlemindedness takes the form of market imperialism; confronting the democratic state, they are advocates of privatization and laissez-faire. Their ideal is a society in which all goods and services are provided by entrepreneurs to consumers. That some entrepreneurs would fail and many consumers find themselves helpless in the marketplace—this is the price of individual autonomy. It is, obviously, a price we already pay: in all capitalist societies, the market makes for inequality. The more successful its imperialism, the greater the inequality. But were the market to be set firmly within civil society, politically constrained, open to communal as well as private initiatives, limits might be fixed on its unequal outcomes. The exact nature of the limits would depend on the strength and density of the associational networks (including, now, the political community).

The problem with inequality is not merely that some individuals are more capable, others less capable, of making their consumer preferences effective. It's not that some individuals live in fancier apartments than others, or drive better-made cars, or take vacations in more exotic places. These are conceivably the just rewards of market success. The problem is that the inequality commonly translates into domination and radical deprivation. But the verb "translates" here describes a socially mediated process, which is fostered or inhibited by the structure of its mediations. Dominated and deprived individuals are likely to be disorganized as well as impoverished, whereas poor people with strong families, churches, unions, political parties, and ethnic alliances are not likely to be dominated or deprived for long. Nor need these people stand alone even in the marketplace. The capitalist answer assumes that the good life of entrepreneurial initiative and consumer choice is a life led most importantly by individuals. But civil society encompasses or can encompass a variety of market agents: family businesses, publicly owned or municipal companies, worker communes, consumer cooperatives, nonprofit organizations of many different sorts. All these function in the market even though they have their origins outside. And just as the experience of democracy is expanded and enhanced by groups that are in but not of the state, so consumer choice is expanded and enhanced by groups that are in but not of the market.

It is only necessary to add that among the groups in but not of the state are market organizations, and among the groups in but not of the market are state organizations. All social forms are relativized by the civil society argument—and on the actual ground too. This also means that all social forms are contestable; moreover, contests can't be won by invoking one or another account of the preferred setting—as if it were enough to say that market organizations, insofar as they are efficient, don't have to be democratic or that state firms, insofar as they are democratically controlled, don't have to operate within the constraints of the market. The exact character of our associational life is something that has to be argued about, and it is in the course of these arguments that we also decide about the forms of democracy, the nature of work, the extent and effects of market inequalities, and much else.

The quality of nationalism is also determined within civil society, where national groups coexist and overlap with families and religious communities (two social formations largely neglected in modernist answers to the question about the good life) and where nationalism is expressed in schools and movements, organizations for mutual aid, cultural and historical societies. It is because groups like these are entangled with other groups, similar in kind but different in aim, that civil society holds out the hope of a domesticated nationalism. In states dominated by a single nation, the multiplicity of the groups pluralizes nationalist politics and culture; in states with more than one nation, the density of the networks prevents radical polarization.

Civil society as we know it has its origins in the struggle for religious freedom. Though often violent, the struggle held open the possibility of peace. "The establishment of this one thing," John Locke wrote about toleration, "would take away all ground of complaints and tumults upon account of conscience." One can easily imagine groundless complaints and tumults, but Locke believed (and he was largely right) that tolerance would dull the edge of religious conflict. People would be less ready to take risks once the stakes were lowered. Civil society simply is that place where the stakes are lower, where, in principle at least, coercion is used only to keep the peace and all associations are equal under the law. In the market, this formal equality often has no substance, but in the world of faith and identity, it is real enough. Though nations don't compete for members in the same way as religions (sometimes) do, the argument for granting them the associational freedom of civil society is similar. When they are free to celebrate their histories, remember their dead, and shape (in part) the education of their children, they are more likely to be harmless than when they are unfree. Locke may have put the claim too strongly when he wrote, "There is only one thing which gathers people into seditious commotions, and that is oppression," but he was close enough to the truth to warrant the experiment of radical tolerance.

But if oppression is the cause of seditious commotion, what is the cause of oppression? I don't doubt that there is a materialist story to tell here, but I want to stress the central role played by ideological single-mindedness: the intolerant universalism of (most) religions, the exclusivity of (most) nations. The actual experience of civil society, when it can be had, seems to work against these two. Indeed, it works so well, some observers think, that neither religious faith nor national identity is likely to survive for long in the network of free associations. But we really don't know to what extent faith and identity depend upon coercion or whether they can reproduce themselves under conditions of freedom. I suspect that they both respond to such deep human needs that they will outlast their current organizational forms. It seems, in any case, worthwhile to wait and see.

Still a Need for State Power

But there is no escape from power and coercion, no possibility of choosing, like the old anarchists, civil society alone. A few years ago, in a book called *Anti-Politics*, the Hungarian dissident George Konrad described a way of living alongside the totalitarian state but, so to speak, with one's back turned toward it. He urged his fellow dissidents to reject the very idea of seizing or sharing power and to devote their energies to religious, cultural, economic, and professional associations. Civil society appears in his book as an alternative to the state, which he assumes to be unchangeable and irredeemably hostile. His argument seemed right to me when I first read his book. Looking back, after the collapse of the communist regimes in Hungary and elsewhere, I can easily see how much it was a product of its time—and how short that time was! No state can survive for long if it is wholly alienated from civil society. It cannot outlast its own coercive machinery; it is lost, literally, without its firepower. The production and reproduction of loyalty, civility, political competence, and trust in authority are never the work of the state alone, and the effort to go it alone—one meaning of totalitarianism—is doomed to failure.

The failure, however, has carried with it terrible costs, and so one can understand the appeal of contemporary antipolitics. Even as central and east European dissidents take power, they remain, and should remain, cautious and apprehensive about its uses. The totalitarian project has left behind an abiding sense of bureaucratic brutality. Here was the ultimate form of political singlemindedness, and though the "democratic" (and, for that matter, the "communist") ideology that they appropriated was false, the intrusions even of a more genuine democracy are rendered suspect by the memory. Post-totalitarian politicians and writers have, in addition, learned the older antipolitics of free enterprise—so that the laissez-faire market is defended in the East today as one of the necessary institutions of civil society, or, more strongly, as the dominant social formation. This second view takes on plausibility from the extraordinary havoc wrought by totalitarian economic "planning." But it rests, exactly like political singlemindedness, on a failure to recognize the pluralism of associational life. The first view leads, often, to a more interesting and more genuinely liberal mistake: it suggests that pluralism is self-sufficient and self-sustaining.

This is, indeed, the experience of the dissidents: the state could not destroy their unions, churches, free universities, illegal markets, *samizdat* publications. Nonetheless, I want to warn against the antipolitical tendencies that commonly accompany the celebration of civil society. The network of associations incorporates, but it cannot dispense with, the agencies of state power; neither can socialist cooperation or capitalist competition dispense with the state. That's why so many dissidents are ministers now. It is indeed true that the new social movements in the East and the West—concerned with ecology, feminism, the rights of immigrants and national minorities, workplace and product safety, and so on—do not aim, as the democratic and labor movements once aimed, at taking power. This represents an important change, in sensibility as much as in ideology, reflecting a new valuation of parts over wholes and a new willingness to settle for something less than total victory. But there can be no victory at all that doesn't involve some control over, or use of, the state apparatus. The collapse of totalitarianism is empowering for the members of civil society precisely because it renders the state accessible.

Here, then, is the paradox of the civil society argument. Citizenship is one of the many roles that members play, but the state itself is unlike all the other associations. It both frames civil society and occupies space within it. It fixes the boundary conditions and the basic rules of all associational activity (including political activity). It compels association members to think about a common good, beyond their own conceptions of the good life. Even the failed totalitarianism of, say, the Polish communist state had this much impact upon the Solidarity union: it determined that Solidarity was a Polish union, focused on economic arrangements and labor policy within the borders of Poland. A democratic state, which is continuous with the other associations, has at the same time a greater say about their quality and vitality. It serves, or it doesn't serve, the needs of the associational networks as these are worked out by men and women who are simultaneously members and citizens. I shall give only a few obvious examples, drawn from American experience.

Families with working parents need state help in the form of publicly funded daycare and effective public schools. National minorities need help in organizing and sustaining their own educational programs. Worker-owned companies and consumer cooperatives need state loans or loan guarantees; so do (even more often) capitalist entrepreneurs and firms. Philanthropy and mutual aid, churches and private universities, depend upon tax exemptions. Labor unions need legal recognition and guarantees against "unfair labor practices." Professional associations need state support for their licensing procedures. And across the entire range of association, individual men and women need to be protected against the power of officials, employers, experts, party bosses, factory foremen, directors, priests, parents, patrons; and small and weak groups need to be protected against large and powerful ones. For civil society, left to itself, generates radically unequal power relationships, which only state power can challenge.

Civil society also challenges state power, most importantly when associations have resources or supporters abroad: world religions, pan-national movements, the new environmental groups, multinational corporations. We are likely to feel differently about these challenges, especially after we recognize the real but relative importance of the state. Multinational corporations, for example, need to be constrained, much like states with imperial ambitions; and the best constraint probably lies in collective security, that is, in alliances with other states that give economic regulation some international effect. The same mechanism may turn out to be useful to the new environmental groups. In the first case, the state pressures the corporation; in the second it responds to environmentalist pressure. The two cases suggest, again, that civil society requires political agency. And the state is an indispensable agent—even if the associational networks also, always, resist the organizing impulses of state bureaucrats.

Only a democratic state can create a democratic civil society; only a democratic society can sustain a democratic state. The civility that makes democratic politics possible can only be learned in the associational networks; the roughly equal and widely dispersed capabilities that sustain the networks have to be fostered by the democratic state. Confronted with an overbearing state, citizens, who are also members, will struggle to make room for autonomous associations and market relationships (and also for local governments and decentralized bureaucracies). But the state can never be what it appears to be in liberal theory, a mere framework for civil society. It is also the instrument of the struggle, used to give a particular shape to the common life. Hence citizenship has a certain practical pre-eminence among all our actual and possible memberships. That's not to say that we must be citizens all the time, finding in politics, as Rousseau urged, the greater part of happiness. Most of us will be happier elsewhere, involved only sometimes in affairs of state. But we must have a state open to our sometime involvement.

Nor need we be involved all the time in our associations. A democratic civil society is one controlled by its members, not through a single process of self-determination but through a large number of different and uncoordinated processes. These needn't all be democratic, for we are likely to be members of many associations, and we will want some of them to be managed in our interests, but also in our absence. Civil society is sufficiently democratic when in some, at least, of its parts we are able to recognize ourselves as authoritative and responsible participants. States are tested by their capacity to sustain this kind of participation—which is very different from the heroic intensity of Rousseauian citizenship. And civil society is tested by its capacity to produce citizens whose interests, at least sometimes, reach farther than themselves and their comrades, who look after the political community that fosters and protects the associational networks.

In Favor of Inclusiveness

I mean to defend a perspective that might be called, awkwardly, "critical associationalism." I want to join, but I am somewhat uneasy with, the civil society argument. It can't be said that nothing is lost when we give up the single-mindedness of democratic citizenship or socialist cooperation or individual authority or national identity. There was a kind of heroism in those projects—a concentration of energy, a clear sense of direction, an unblinking recognition of friends and enemies. To make one of these one's own was a serious commitment. The defense of civil society doesn't seem quite comparable. Associational engagement is conceivably as important a project as any of the others, but its greatest virtue lies in its inclusiveness, and inclusiveness does not make for heroism. "Join the associations of your choice" is not a slogan to rally political militants. And yet that is what civil society requires: men and women actively engaged—in state, economy, and nation, and also in churches, neighborhoods, and families, and in many other settings too. To reach this goal is not as easy as it sounds; many people, perhaps most people, live very loosely within the networks; a growing number of people seem to be radically disengaged—passive clients of the state, market dropouts, resentful and posturing nationalists. And the civil society project doesn't confront an energizing hostility, as all the others do; its protagonists are more likely to meet sullen indifference, fear, despair, apathy, and withdrawal.

In central and eastern Europe, civil society is still a battle cry, for it requires a dismantling of the totalitarian state and it brings with it the exhilarating experience of associational independence. Among ourselves what is required is nothing so grand; nor does it lend itself to a singular description (but this is what lies ahead in the East too). The civil society project can only be described in terms of all the other projects, against their singularity. Hence my account in these pages, which suggests the need (1) to decentralize the state so that there are more opportunities for citizens to take responsibility for (some of) its activities; (2) to socialize the economy so that there is a great diversity of market agents, communal as well as private; and (3) to pluralize and domesticate nationalism, on the religious model, so that there are different ways to realize and sustain historical identities.

None of this can be accomplished without using political power to redistribute resources and to underwrite and subsidize the most desirable associational activities. But political power alone cannot accomplish any of it. The kinds of "action" discussed by theorists of the state need to be supplemented (not, however, replaced) by something radically different: more like union organizing than political mobilization, more like teaching in a school than arguing in the assembly, more like volunteering in a hospital than joining a political party, more like working in an ethics alliance or feminist support group than canvassing in an election, more like shaping a co-op budget than deciding on national fiscal policy. But can any of these local and small-scale activities ever carry with them the honor of citizenship? Sometimes, certainly they are narrowly conceived, partial and particularist; they need political correction. The greater problem, however, is that they seem so ordinary. Living in civil society, one might think, is like speaking in prose.

But just as speaking in prose implies an understanding of syntax, so these forms of action (when they are pluralized) imply an understanding of civility. And that is not an understanding about which we can be entirely confident these days. There is something to be said for the neoconservative argument that in the modern world we need to recapture the density of associational life and relearn the activities and understandings that go with it. And if this is the case, then a more strenuous argument is called for from the left: we have to reconstruct that same density under new conditions of freedom and equality. It would appear to be an elementary requirement of social democracy that there exist a society of lively, engaged, and effective men and women—where the honor of "action" belongs to the many and not to the few.

Against a background of growing disorganization—violence, homelessness, divorce, abandonment, alienation, and addiction—a society of this sort looks more like a necessary achievement than a comfortable reality. In truth, however, it was never a comfortable reality, except for the few. Most men and women have been trapped in one or another subordinate relationship, where the "civility" they learned was deferential rather than independent and active. That is why democratic citizenship, socialist production, free enterprise, and nationalism were all of them liberating projects. But none of them has yet produced a general, coherent, or sustainable liberation. And their more single-minded adherents, who have exaggerated the effectiveness of the state or the market or the nation and neglected the networks, have probably contributed to the disorder of contemporary life. The projects have to be relativized and brought together, and the place to do that is in civil society, the setting of settings, where each can find the partial fulfillment that is all it deserves.

Civil society itself is sustained by groups much smaller than the demos or the working class or the mass of consumers or the nation. All these are necessarily fragmented and localized as they are incorporated. They become part of the world of family, friends, comrades, and colleagues, where people are connected to one another and made responsible for one another. Connected and responsible: without that, "free and equal" is less attractive than we once thought it would be. I have no magic formula for making connections or strengthening the sense of responsibility. These aren't aims that can be underwritten with historical guarantees or achieved through a single unified struggle. Civil society is a project of projects; it requires many organizing strategies and new forms of state action. It requires a new sensitivity for what is local, specific, contingent—and, above all, a new recognition (to paraphrase a famous sentence) that the good life is in the details.

Select Bibliography

Alinsky, Saul D. 1971. *Rules for Radicals: A Practical Primer for Realistic Radicals.* Random House.

Arato, Andrew, and Jean Cohen. 1992. *Civil Society and Political Theory.* MIT Press.

Barber, Benjamin. 1998. *A Place for Us: How to Make Society Civil and Democracy Strong.* Hill and Wang.

———. 1992. *An Aristocracy of Everyone: The Politics of Education and the Future of America.* Ballantine Books.

Bell, Daniel. 1976. *The Cultural Contradictions of Capitalism.* Basic Books.

Berger, Peter, and Richard John Neuhaus. 1996. *To Empower People.* 2d ed. AEI Press.

Boyte, Harry C., and Nancy Kari. 1996. *Building America: The Democratic Promise of Public Work.* Temple University Press.

Brehm, John, and Wendy Rahn. 1996. "Individual Level Evidence for the Causes and Consequences of Social Capital." Paper presented at a conference sponsored by the Pew Charitable Trust, the National Commission on Civic Renewal, and the Brookings Institution, November 25.

Burke, Edmund. 1961. *Reflections on the Revolution in France.* Doubleday.

Ehrenhalt, Alan. 1996. *The Lost City.* Basic Books.

Etzioni, Amitai. 1996. *The New Golden Rule: Community and Morality in a Democratic Society.* Basic Books.

———. 1993. *The Spirit of Community: Rights, Responsibilities, and the Communitarian Agenda.* Crown Publishers.

Greeley, Andrew. 1972. *Unsecular Man: The Persistence of Religion.* Schocken Books.
———. 1971. *Why Can't They Be Like Us? America's White Ethnic Groups.* Dutton.
Harris, Fredrick C. 1997. "Will the Circle Be Unbroken? The Erosion and Transformation of African–American Civic Life." Paper prepared for the Working Group, National Commission on Civic Renewal, June 20–21.
Ladd, Everett C. 1996. "The Data Just Don't Show Erosion of America's 'Social Capital.'" *Public Perspective* 17 (June–July).
Loury, Glenn C., and Linda Datcher Loury. 1997. "Not by Bread Alone: The Role of the African-American Church in Inner-City Development." *Brookings Review* (Winter): 10–13.
Kotlowitz, Alex. 1991. *There are No Children Here: The Story of Two Boys Growing Up in the Other America.* Doubleday.
Mayer, Susan. *What Money Can't Buy: Family Income and Children's Life Chances.* Harvard University Press, 1997.
Miller, Warren E., and J. Merrill Shanks. 1996. *The New American Voter.* Harvard University Press.
Nisbet, Robert. 1969. *The Quest for Community.* Oxford University.
———. 1970. *Tradition and Revolt.* Vintage Books.
Pettinico, George. 1996. "Civic Participation: Alive and Well in Today's Environmental Groups." *Public Perspective* 7 (June–July).
Pew Research Center for the People and the Press. 1997. "Trust and Citizen Engagement in Metropolitan Philadelphia: A Case Study."
Putnam, Robert. 1995. "Bowling Alone: America's Declining Social Capital." *Journal of Democracy* (January).
Rusk, David. 1993. *Cities without Suburbs.* Woodrow Wilson Center Press.
Salamon, Lester M., and Helmut K. Anheier. 1997. "The Civil Society Sector." *Society* 34 (January-February): 60–65.
Sandel, Michael. 1996. *Democracy's Discontent: America in Search of a Public Philosophy.* Belknap Press of Harvard University Press.
Seligman, Adam. 1992. *The Idea of Civil Society.* Free Press.
Skocpol, Theda . 1996. "Unraveling from Above." *American Prospect* (March–April).
Starobin, Paul. 1997. "Civilizing Capitalism." *National Journal* 29 (January): 106–09.
Uslaner, Eric. 1996. "Social Capital, Television, and the 'Mean World.'" Paper presented at a conference sponsored by the Pew Charitable Trust, the National Commission on Civic Renewal, and the Brookings Institution, November 25.
Verba, Sidney, Kay Lehman Schlozman, and Henry E. Brady. 1995. *Voice and Equality: Civic Voluntarism in American Politics.* Harvard University Press.

Wilson, William J. 1987. *The Truly Disadvantaged: The Inner City, the Underclass, and Public Policy*. University of Chicago Press.

Wolfe, Alan. 1989. *Whose Keeper? Social Science and Moral Obligation*. University of California Press.

———. 1998. *One Nation, After All: What Middle-Class Americans Really Think about God, Country, Family, Racism, Welfare, Immigration, Homosexuality, Work, the Right, the Left, and Each Other.*Viking Press.

Wuthnow, Robert. 1994. *Sharing the Journey: Support Groups and America's New Quest for Community*. Free Press.

Contributors

Bill Bradley has taken on several roles since he left the Senate in 1997. He is currently a visiting professor at Stanford University and chairman of the National Civic League. This essay is adapted from an earlier speech.

Dan Coats is a Republican senator from Indiana.

John J. DiIulio Jr., Douglas Dillon Senior Fellow at the Brookings Institution and professor of politics and public affairs at Princeton University, directs the Partnership for Research on Religion and At-Risk Youth (PRRAY) in Philadelphia, which provides technical assistance and financial support to inner-city youth.

E.J. Dionne Jr. is a syndicated columnist for the *Washington Post* and a senior fellow at the Brookings Institution. He is the author of *They Only Look Dead: Why Progressives Will Dominate the Next Political Era* and *Why Americans Hate Politics.*

Alan Ehrenhalt is executive editor of *Governing* magazine. His chapter first appeared in his book, *The Lost City: Discovering the Forgotten Virtues of Community in the Chicago of the 1950s* (Basic Books, 1995), pp. 17–27. Reprinted by permission of HarperCollins.

Jane R. Eisner is editorial page editor of the *Philadelphia Inquirer.*

Jean Bethke Elshtain, Laura Spelman Rockefeller Professor of Social and Political Ethics at the University of Chicago, is the author of *Democracy on Trial* (Basic Books, 1995).

William A. Galston is director of the Institute for Philosophy and Public Policy at the University of Maryland. He is executive director of the National Commission on Civic Renewal. The views expressed in the article by him and Peter Levine are theirs alone and not those of the National Commission, its members, or its scholarly advisers.

Gertrude Himmelfarb is the author of *The De-moralization of Society: From Victorian Virtues to Modern Values* (Alfred Knopf, 1995). Her essay is reprinted with permission; it originally appeared in the September 9, 1996, issue of the *Weekly Standard.*

Bruce Katz is director of the Brookings Center on Urban and Metropolitan Policy and a senior fellow in the Brookings Economic Studies program.

David Kuo is president of the American Compass.

Peter Levine is a research scholar at the Institute for Philosophy and Public Policy at the University of Maryland and deputy director of the National Commission on Civic Renewal. The views expressed in the article by him and William A. Galston are theirs alone and not those of the National Commission, its members, or its scholarly advisers.

Colin L. Powell was chairman of the U.S. Joint Chiefs of Staff from 1989 to 1993. He was general chairman of the Presidents' Summit for America's Future, which met in Philadelphia, April 27–29, 1997, and is chairman of its successor organization, America's Promise—the Alliance for Youth.

Gail Pressberg is a senior fellow at the Institute for Civil Society.

Eugene F. Rivers III is pastor of the Azusa Christian Community in Boston, Massachusetts, and codirector of the National Ten-Point Leadership Foundation.

Rick Santorum is a Republican senator from Pennsylvania.

William A. Schambra is director of general programs for the Lynde and Harry Bradley Foundation in Milwaukee, Wisconsin. His article is adapted from a paper presented to the National Commission on Civic Renewal in Washington, D.C., on January 25, 1997.

Theda Skocpol is professor of government and sociology at Harvard University. Her article is adapted from testimony presented before the National Commission on Civic Renewal in Washington, D.C., on January 25, 1997.

Pam Solo is president of the Institute for Civil Society.

Michael Walzer is professor of social science at the Institute for Advanced Study in Princeton, N.J. His essay is reprinted with permission; it originally appeared in the Spring 1991 issue of *Dissent.*

Alan Wolfe is professor of sociology at Boston University. He is the author of *Whose Keeper? Social Science and Moral Obligation* (University of California Press, 1989) and *One Nation, After All* (Viking/Penguin, 1998).

Index